Graffiti at Ravelrig House prior to restoration

PHOTOGRAPHY AND ILLUSTRATIONS

We are grateful to the following people and organisations for the use of the photographs and images in this book:

B. Allen, Allies & Morrison, The Architects Journal, Andrew Baxter, Angus Bremner, Building Design, Oliver Chapman, Ted Cullinan Architects, Cumming Architects, David Churchill, Alan Crumlish, CZWG, Dolan & Donnelly Architects, Alan Forbes, Gavin Fraser, F. Genin O Lacau & M.L. Fantino, GM+AD, Graphic Partners, Graven Images, Richard Horden Associates, Gareth Hoskins, Alastair Hunter, Keith Hunter, Rob Hunter, Jon Jardine, Eva Jiricna Architects, Kinnear Crotch, Andrew Lee, MBNA, David Miller, Richard Murphy, Allan Murray Architects, Tina Norris, Photogenic, Pink Zepplin, Pixel, Antonia Reeve, Philip Charles Rider, Van Rijn Vago Architects with Chris Clark Associates & Ling Chegli, RMJM, Machiel Spaan & Berend Van Der Lans, Morley Von Sternberg, Sutherland Hussey, Troughton McAslan, Mike Williamson, Stephen Wiltshire M.B.E. Michael Wolchover, Mr Wyatt

First published 2007 by
Neil Baxter Associates, Glasgow

Text: the contributors
Design: Jon Jardine (mail@jonjardine.com)

ISBN: 978-0-9537149-4-0

A catalogue record for this book is available from the British Library

Contents

Foreword

Neil Baxter

THIS BOOK HAS BEEN three years in the making. The original brief from John Forbes and Andy Burrell sought a narrative that would record quarter of a century of achievement, alongside learned essays, commentary and anecdote from friends and associates, project profiles and a comprehensive catalogue. They also required a volume rich in images, both drawn and photographic. In development terms this was a complex mix of uses to fit into one, relatively modest, site.

Working with the Burrell team has been challenging, frustrating, stimulating and, ultimately, rewarding. There can be no doubt that these words and images chart the evolution of one of Scotland's most remarkable businesses, a development company which has profoundly influenced the design of Scotland's cities.

The photographers who have recorded the achievements of The Burrell Company and its architects provide a visual record which powerfully demonstrates the ingenuity, innovation and quality of their subjects. Jon Jardine's design draws all of this material together in a volume which elegantly portrays a quarter century of achievement which has re-shaped Scotland's urban landscape.

Neil Baxter, August 2007

Preface

Professor Andy MacMillan and Professor Isi Metzstein

TRUE ARCHITECT/DEVELOPERS ARE rare indeed. A strange hybrid of architectural passion allied to money, presumably borrowed at high rates of interest, they are concerned with how their buildings look, how they fit within their context, how well they function and that all this should help them sell. Yet they are fleeting creatures. All too often, like caterpillar to butterfly, only in reverse, they undergo the sad transformation through the chrysalis phase of developer/architect then, ultimately, to a lower, mercenary form, only concerned with the bottom line.

Andy Burrell, John Forbes and their cohorts are an extraordinary phenomenon. The combined genius of Mr. Burrell and the late, great, Andy Doolan created a unique development model. Their enthusiasm and insight anticipated the shift in emphasis of the 1980s from new-build on the periphery of Scotland's cities towards re-inhabiting what remained of the fragmented fabric of Edinburgh's and Glasgow's city centres. Then they started to fill the gaps in between.

In 25 years of continuous achievement The Burrell Company have commissioned many young designers now recognised as among the finest of Scotland's architects. They have altered expectations by providing ingeniously planned and beautiful dwellings with good standards of finish in refurbished buildings. They commission extraordinary buildings on sites overlooked or rejected by others of lesser vision and often mix uses, retail, offices, creative space and residential, all in the one block.

The Burrell Company's work, both directly and by influencing and encouraging, has improved Scottish architecture immeasurably. Perhaps their most notable achievement has been to raise the expectation of buyers. By example they have greatly enhanced the overall quality of urban development.

Often The Burrell Company have struggled against the limited vision of planners and those who have tried to thwart their ambitions or steal their ideas. Yet their drive, vision and determination has delivered a rich range of projects of which they and their architects can be proud. And somehow they manage to retain their enthusiasm and an infectious sense of fun. Those who have had the privilege of joining Messrs Burrell, Forbes, Ross and the rest of the team to celebrate acquisitions, competitions, launches and completions will certainly testify to that.

The Burrell Company have spent a quarter of a century changing Scottish urban architecture for the better, educating planners, politicians and the public on the benefits of good design and creating opportunities for innovative architects. They have remained a rare creature indeed; the persisting, enlightened architect/developer. And long may they continue.

The International Context

Hugh Pearman

YOU CAN NEVER SAY for sure that any urban or architectural movement began at a given time and place. It is even less possible to state with conviction when a consensus view – nationally or internationally - was agreed. Some architectural historians are very keen to establish such moments, but social historians know that things are always a lot less tidy than that. The squirming city, which is as much organic as man-made, resists easy categorisation and control.

Nonetheless, broad trends become apparent. One very protracted moment in the history of Western cities was, and is, the uncomfortable shift from industrial to post-industrial; from the city as manufacturing base to the city as – what? City of Culture? City of tourism? City of service industries? Or city as depopulating centre, good only for demolition, with no revitalising plan on the horizon?

Bad old habits die hard. The Government's current "Pathfinder" initiative for the north of England is little more than a rebranded version of the old, discredited notion of slum clearance. That essentially Victorian philosophy – there's a problem, so let's tackle the symptoms rather than the causes - prevailed right up to the 1970s, and it took a growing resistance movement to stop it then. That, and the opportunity that a new breed of developer saw in some of the old buildings. This is where The Burrell Company came in.

The opportunities that presented themselves in Britain's industrial towns and cities were not always enlightened refurbishment. There was a point in the 1980s when an abandoned mill or warehouse building in Lancashire was valuable only as a source of salvageable building materials, to be used on the new shopping centres then being built in the South. Even that was better than nothing: a negative value on these buildings was not uncommon. And then there are all the goods yards and stock yards and gasworks and wharfs, the hectares of contaminated soil. These things take time. Even in London, the larger defunct industrial areas, such as King's Cross or the Greenwich Peninsula, are only now starting to show real regeneration progress.

But there was a time, in the late 1970s, when the national and international mood turned from the old idea of "comprehensive redevelopment" to more of a creative-repair approach. Conservationists had argued the merits of better industrial buildings since the 1950s. Even free-enterprise America was starting to find new uses for some of its prettier industrial buildings, in Boston and San Francisco, for instance. London's Covent Garden Market followed suit in the 1980s. And an interesting mix of architectural interests – firebrand conservationists from Left and Right, plus some small entrepreneurial developers – started to find ways to reinhabit the abandoned bits of our cities.

As Andy Burrell has observed, this growing mood of urban reappraisal coincided with a loosening of the rules as to what architects were allowed to do. Henceforth they could be developers as well as designers. The people with good ideas could build them for themselves, assuming they could source the money. In truth there were never very many such architect-developers, but what they have tended to do is blaze a trail that the men in suits could follow. And it is certainly true that, in Thatcher's Britain, with the public sector being pared back, a lot of architects had to become more development-minded just to survive.

Different cities evolve at different speeds. In redevelopment terms, Leeds today is where Manchester was ten years ago, while Bradford, for instance, is a further decade behind that. Newcastle/Gateshead does things differently, but is working on broadly the Manchester timescale, as is Bristol. But before Manchester came Glasgow. And in Glasgow, a company called Kantel, forerunner of The Burrell Company, came to prominence with its Ingram Square development. Occupying an entire city block in the then run-down Merchant City, mixing new and refurbished architecture, the significance and influence of Ingram Square cannot be overstated.

This is one of those developments that you look at now and think – what was all the fuss about? Obvious, isn't it? And stylistically it has, of course dated, though not too badly. It has its postmodernist touches. That, however, is irrelevant: it's the planning that counts, the making of a three-dimensional jigsaw puzzle, the mix of uses, the blend of public and private spaces, the deployment of artists working alongside architects. These are ingredients that have stood the test of time. As a venture it was more natural than the slightly frantic assemblage of forms you find in the "Homes for the Future" development that came out of the Glasgow '99 year of architecture and design, in which The Burrell Company was heavily involved. But that too was important as a signal of what could be done. It was all about raising ambitions.

In the city regeneration game, there are wide variations. In West Berlin before reunification, for instance, a lot of redevelopment was down to tax breaks: essentially, people had to be paid to live there. But there as elsewhere, it was artists and boho types who found the best and cheapest areas to colonise, establishing a bridgehead for later developers. And then, once the Wall came down, the same started to happen in the former Eastern sector district of Prenzlauerberg. Arguably the piecemeal uplift there, block by 19th century block, was a more genuine kind of city-making than the simultaneous state-organised rebuild-fest along the line of the Wall. A better example of the public-sector-led approach would, of course, be Barcelona. The achievements of that city are certainly over-praised, but it cannot be faulted – any more than Bilbao – for engaging seriously with the transition from industrial centre to cultural honeypot. When you start having to build new airports to handle a massive growth in visitors, you know that something is going right.

In New York – Manhattan to be exact – new ex-industrial areas were being rediscovered one by one. Where Andy Warhol and the Velvet Underground had ventured, others followed and the original "loft living" culture proved highly exportable. New York however remains unusual in North America: the dead downtowns, run-down ghettos and abandoned riverside industrial areas of a city such as Cincinnati is unfortunately more usually the picture. At least

efforts are now beginning there and elsewhere to correct the mistakes of the post-war years.

In continental Europe, nobody needed too much persuading of the merits of living in city centres. It was another matter entirely in Britain, especially England with its ingrained suburban ethos. Scotland's tradition of high-density tenement living had never much appealed to the English. By the early 1980s, very few people indeed lived in the centres of Birmingham or Manchester: the lights went out when the offices and shops closed and the commuters disappeared to the urban fringes. Although the picture was healthier north of the border, Glasgow's decaying trading centre and Edinburgh's Old Town were starting to fall into ruin. What first Kantel and then its successors, including The Burrell Company, did was to scent the opportunity the existing fabric presented. The culture of knocking down awkward old buildings was still strong and to some extent remains strong: but by imaginatively recasting old buildings in both cities, adding new ones, and by proving that there was a strong untapped demand for apartments in the centres of those cities, Burrell showed what could and should be done.

I think the difference is this. There are enlightened non-architect developers, of course, and then there are your average developers – the majority. These like to start with a clean sheet, or at any rate a straightforward proposition. Sweep the awkward stuff away and rebuild, or do a simple conversion, take the money and run. Until recently, monocultural uses were preferred – offices here, housing there, retail somewhere else. A formula was, and often still is, applied that both planners and financiers will be familiar with. The better developers try harder, but they can't help themselves: they still like to scrape clean, sterilise, and rebuild. Local authorities also like the clean-sheet approach because it is highly visible. By sanctioning this, they can be seen to be doing something on a grand scale.

But architects, if they are any good, think differently from standard developers and local authorities. They like their

complexity and contradiction. They get a perverse pleasure in finding ingenious ways to make old buildings live again, especially with a mix of uses. Of course they like to build new, but they also like to bounce off the old. Plenty of cutting-edge architects do their best work in a historical context. And by doing this, they add value.

So when you get a developer who is also an architect, the result may very well be a more complex, more time-consuming but ultimately more rewarding kind of development: often in a fringe area that a conventional developer would not touch. For me, what comes through in the work of The Burrell Company is a strong sense of urban continuity. They do not necessarily destroy in order to rebuild, and when they do build new they understand better how the urban realm evolves continually. It is as damaging to a city to engage in slavish historicism as it is to suddenly declare swathes of its perfectly good buildings redundant. The character of a place, its layers of history and meaning, are delicate things to mess with. It is usually better to perform surgery than to give up and declare the patient dead.

Beyond this, The Burrell Company has brought on a phalanx of good young – now middle-aged – architects. In a way you can compare it to the Temple Bar organisation in Dublin, which rescued that evocative city district from being swept away in the name of progress. Progress was achieved by other means, by architects and developers sharing the same view, by planning, converting and rebuilding intelligently and with passion. In this case two cities were involved but you can argue that the catalytic effect of The Burrell Company and their architects is similarly wide-ranging. By showing how it can be done, it can be done. It is as simple – and as difficult – as that.

Hugh Pearman is architecture and design critic of The Sunday Times and author of books including Contemporary World Architecture, published by Phaidon, and Airports: a century of architecture, published by Laurence King.

The Scottish Context

Charles McKean

WHEN THE CONSERVATIVE GOVERNMENT compelled the architectural institutes to radicalise their definition and practices of professionalism in March 1981, there were dire predictions about the likely consequences for architecture. Allowing architects to compete on fees would, they said, favour the larger practices at the expense of the medium and that, to some extent, has transpired. It would also drive down, they said, the amount of time architects spent designing, and thereby lower the quality of the building. That proved correct as well, in many cases – although significant architects continued to invest the necessary design time, at their own expense. Allowing architects the freedom to market their services was greeted with the fear that the profession would vulgarise itself – which has been the case only really with the usual suspects.

Permitting architects to be builders and developers whilst remaining architects and members of the institutes was more problematic. Most architects understood that having a fellow architect inside the client body should bring greater understanding of what the architect was trying to achieve culturally to the client team than was normally the case; but they feared lest clients might be misled about which advice was professionally objective, and which influenced by self-interest. The Royal Incorporation of Architects in Scotland's take on this was more sophisticated than that of the UK big sister institute, the Royal Institute of British Architects. RIAS members were to be judged retrospectively, according to whether a client could demonstrate that there had been either an undisclosed or an unresolved conflict of interest. If not, then the Scots were at liberty to branch out.

Some months before the appointed date, Andy Doolan and Andy Burrell appeared in the RIAS, determined to set up as architect developers and seeking legitimacy. They were the first to receive formal permission to do so in Scotland. Despite expectations that many others would follow, they didn't.

The profession's expectation of architect-developers was high. Architectural quality of development would improve through the architect-developer applying a quality threshold in place of the 'bottom line', being prepared to take whatever risks a good project required, and being able to conceive of non-standard and imaginative solutions to development problems. Above all, architects hoped that designers would be selected on the grounds of architectural quality.

Retrospectively, much of this can be seen as wishful thinking by a profession that perpetually conceives of itself as being under threat. Nonetheless, the pointilliste trajectory chosen by The Burrell Company, with its carefully selected sites and strong showing in heritage property rescue and conversion, was not what most of the profession had in mind when using the term 'architect-developer'. Their preoccupation was with those who spawned speculative office blocks or the sea of poor-value, miserable speculative housing vomited upon our urban boundaries. These easy markets, sadly, were more than profitable without the need to engage with architecture or architect-directors. The Burrell saga implies that an architect-developer has to develop niche markets to survive.

What kind of niche markets? Once Kantel and The Burrell Company split, the latter developed a stream of projects similar to that of a miniature Phoenix Trust – namely taking over buildings in former institutional use and converting them – usually into apartments. In some cases, the building was in considerable difficulty. Duddingston House, for example, a hotel rapidly sinking into despond, might have become vulnerable to vandalism and fire, as had happened to so many others of Edinburgh's unwanted great villas. The half-demolished Tailors' Hall Court in the Cowgate, the last Renaissance Trade Guildhall left in Edinburgh, was neglected as a University store.

Most of Burrell's work to date has been restricted to the hinterland of Scotland's two largest cities, although they have now expanded into Aberdeen. There was a single abortive project in Dundee, where they took a scunner to the lack of vision among the councillors fifteen years ago. They have achieved nothing there, which is tragic, given its wealth of really ancient properties in need of a future.

Although Edinburgh and Glasgow have the largest markets, they also have the greatest developer competition. This has forced Burrell to play to its principal strengths: having the design imagination of two architects in-house able to challenge the design advice of their carefully selected consultant architects, enabling them to think small on a large scale and vice versa. The result is that projects emerge from a broader range of options than is normally the case. Thus they have given problem sites and complex buildings a well-designed new life that works commercially. In a sense, that says it all. That is what vindicates architect developers.

Burrell needed the most creative advice and the most flexible partners. What is striking about its record is not the occasional ordinary development and associated humdrum architect (for it has not been wholly exempt from that), but its unmatched portfolio of quality architects with quality projects: Elder and Cannon, Simister Monaghan, Reiach and Hall, the late Rob Hunter, Richard Murphy, Allan Murray, Page and Park, Ted Cullinan, Davis Duncan, John McAslan, Campbell Zogolovitch Wilkinson and Gough, Richard Horden, Ushida Findlay, Lee Boyd, Richard Reid, Gareth Hoskins, Parr Shearer, RMJM Glasgow, Malcolm Fraser, Sutherland Hussey and others.

If The Burrell Company had been perceived as exploitative in its approach, such architects would not have worked with it. That it is a developer operating at constant risk which has commissioned such architects should put local authorities, housing associations, the Government and the Universities, with all their secure funding, to shame.

One of the appointment mechanisms Burrell has used has been architectural competition. In the case of the Glasgow Tower (not built on the site in St Enoch's Square for which it was designed) and the abortive Fettes Lodge they issued open invitations. The latter, held to coincide with the RIAS' 150th birthday party in 1990, was particularly popular,

and the sadly abortive winner by David Miller was a stern jeu d'esprit which would have added much to north Edinburgh.

The competitive selection process for Coalhill and Ronaldson's Wharf in Leith resulted in two of the most striking new developments in the revival of that ancient port. To enter the developer competition for Edinburgh's Morrison Street, The Burrell Company joined Argent, from London, and the elegant eliptical urban design they commissioned together from Edward Cullinan, based upon a contemporary interpretation of Grosvenor Crescent, was the most distinguished entry. It is now almost 20 years later, and the site remains a car park – which implies that there had been other agendas for the site undisclosed at the time.

The world of the developer - architect or not - is one of taking risks. Just as most institutional clients tend to be risk-averse, most developers attempt to limit their risks. To them, it is a method of processing money through the medium of building. Risk-free development opportunities, therefore, would all have been seized by standard developers long before The Burrell Company had got wind of them. So, in addition to the normal developer's financial risks, The Burrell Company has had to tackle additional risk – the social and physical risks inherent in their selected sites and buildings, and any risk consequent upon appointing architects who were not normal 'developer's architects'.

Most frequently, Burrell has taken a chance upon social attitudes changing. It was Kantel rather than Glasgow Council that prepared the overall vision regenerating the Merchant City, of which Ingram Square was only a part, at a time when that district of old Glasgow was anathema to developers. When Burrell then undertook Old Assembly Close in Edinburgh's High Street, the then City Director of Estates, Bob Mackintosh, opined that 'nobody nice' would like to live in the Old Town. That was the official established wisdom.

Old Assembly Close was one of the first projects in the revival of the High Street and Old Town; and it was symbolic that Burrell opened a street-front office right there – in what,

at that time, was still a profoundly unfashionable location good only for tourist tat and the Fringe. A developer seeking solely to make money would not have taken it on.

Burrell took a comparable chance in the Park Circus area of Glasgow, by converting Park School into fashionable, high-quality apartments at a time when nobody was buying smart flats in a district still regarded coolly by unimaginative estate agents; and the RIAS competition for flats on an adjacent site had been aborted for that very reason. Nor had anybody believed that really expensive flats would sell in run-down Leith, given the difficulties encountered by those who converted the north end of the Vaults or the then stuttering sales at the Cooperage; and it was a brave venture for all of those involved in the Homes for the Future, off Glasgow Green.

Indeed, from time to time, Burrell has built substantially ahead of the market, as proved to be the case at Carrick Quay flats on the banks of the Clyde in central Glasgow. Some of the highest risk schemes were those with highest profile which indicates that the 'loss-leader' calculation may have played a part in the assessment. Nonetheless, once Burrell had started the process, it tended to prove easier for those that followed.

Burrell, and their partners, eventually restored most of the south side of Edinburgh's High Street between Hunter Square and Parliament Square, in the course of which they have successfully inserted a smart new office for themselves, and two of Edinburgh's most striking contemporary buildings into a setting of incomparable heritage value. The site in Fishmarket Close, a regional council car park, had been suggested for an 'air rights' architectural competition by the RIAS back in the 1980s since it lay within a few feet of Edinburgh's celebrated 12-storey 'great tenement,' burned down in 1821. Nobody – the Council, the Old Town Renewal Trust, or developers – had been enthusiastic, scared by the novelty of the concept, and by the complexities of constructing a 7-8 storeyed narrow building in a tight urban location.

Burrell, by contrast, relishes such difficult and prominent sites. It also relishes the challenge of equally prominent and equally difficult pieces of the heritage: nowhere more prominent than Allan Ramsay's Goosepie House on the brow of Edinburgh's Castle Hill, with its John Duncan murals. This was the heart of Patrick Geddes' alternative University - University Hall – which he located in Ramsay's Garden. With their associations and cultural memories, old buildings like these carry additional risks – not least the risk that earlier owners had undertaken unrecorded structural alterations which in this case became all too apparent once work began.

Taking risks has financial consequences. Of Burrell's 60 pre-2005 projects, 25% never came to fruition, and 10-15% more at least lost money or ran into other kinds of trouble. Prominent in Burrell's perception are the difficulties caused by planners, and planning committees. The Burrell Company had considerable impatience with the poor calibre of planning they encountered in Dundee. There the approach favoured standard developers with standard sites to produce a bare minimum rather than be more radical. Looking at the Burrell design stable, and comparing that to the quality of recent developer design in Dundee, one can see that Burrell and Co have a point.

The projects pursued by The Burrell Company over the years reflect Andy Burrell's own principal interests – which are exemplified by his having trained as a modern architect, and yet devoting great energy to being chairman of the Cockburn Conservation Trust. He and his colleague, John Forbes, particularly enjoy transforming historic buildings to a contemporary use. They relish the conjunction of old and new as exemplified in their own offices. The Burrell approach has, therefore, been 'to keep as much of the old as possible,' and juxtapose it with contemporary work. The consequence has been that significant pieces of Scottish heritage have been adapted (rather than 'restored') to remarkable new uses: a church to a piping centre, a hostel to stunning des. res., a school to elegant apartments. Mr Burrell's erstwhile

cohort, Mr Doolan, transformed a bank into an inn, and a derelict store into an hotel and pub/restaurant.

Where order has to be brought to a disordered building like the Tailor's Hall, partnerships are required, and a singular Burrell success has been nurturing development partners to back unusual or extraordinary projects. Whereas it is curious that they have not had any partnerships with, say, The National Trust for Scotland Little Houses Scheme, or with any of Scotland's 28 Building Preservation Trusts, most of what The Burrell Company is now achieving is in partnership with other developers. These have been more 'normal' developers, who probably would never have contemplated any of these sites, nor any of the architects Burrell selected. They have done so because Burrell's proven track record demonstrates the added value of appointing clever and ingenious designers to turn the impossible into the possible. Taking this niche approach more deeply into the mainstream development world is, perhaps, The Burrell Company's most distinctive achievement.

Has Burrell's activities over the last 25 years altered attitudes? Undoubtedly in some cases, since built examples of award-winning new-build in sensitive settings, and imaginative adaptation of the heritage provide object lessons difficult to ignore. However, it is not clear that all local authorities are fully alert to the opportunities added by excellent design. Indeed, they may be less so than twenty years ago, with the loss of their design teams and removal of city architects. The very limited geographical spread of Burrell projects implies that too many still consider themselves, like tinpot kings, sufficient in themselves. Looking at what they build shows how hollow that claim is.

Nonetheless, when considering outstanding historic areas desperate for treatment – like the Victoria Road complex in Dundee – Burrell has shown what can be done – but possibly only by Burrell. Burrell's influence on new build derives from its striking if inconsistent patronage of clever designers, but there is little evidence that its lead is being much followed by others. What it has done is showcased

talent – but much is now of a certain age. Just as the design stable was built up, in part, as the result of competitions, perhaps new small-scale competitions would admit new talent.

An unusually high proportion of Burrell Company or Burrell partnership projects are now on the architectural tourist trail – far more than for any other developer projects in Scotland. The only other parallels are in London where the Peabody Trust, for example, with infinitely greater resources and a much simpler purpose, followed a similar trajectory under their architect-trained, former Development Director, Dickon Robinson. That Scotland can be proud of Ingram Square, The Tron, Coalhill, Carrick Quay, Dublin Colonies, Homes for the Future and Upper Strand – in their own way, all pioneering in urban terms showing a particular sensitivity and empathy to their locations – is down to two small private companies and their partners.

The liberation of March 1981 made this possible. For Scots, it should be chastening to realise that, with Andy Doolan's death, The Burrell Company is the only one of its kind.

Charles McKean is Professor of Scottish Architectural History at Dundee University. He is author of The Scottish Thirties, The Making of the Museum of Scotland, The Scottish Chateau and author and editor of numerous architectural guidebooks.

A Life in
Buildings

A Life in Buildings – A Reminiscence

Andrew Burrell

IF MEMORY SERVES ME RIGHT, the change in the rules to allow architects to act as developers was discussed during the late 1970s. The architectural profession had imposed the ruling that architects couldn't act as developers way back – I think during the 1930s. Quite why I can't say as there are plenty of historic precedents of architects acting as developers from Adam to Lorimer. There were quite a few people lobbying for change and the absurd rule was abolished early in 1981 – at least north of the border.

Scotland was ahead of England in this regard, and it was the Royal Incorporation of Architects in Scotland and not the Royal Institute of British Architects who really took the lead. Once the RIBA saw what was happening in Scotland they got their own act together. I think they changed their rules a year or so later.

My reasons for wanting to see a change in the regulations were straightforward. My friend Andy Doolan and I had recently qualified. We were both keen to start righting all sorts of architectural wrongs, as we saw them. We had considered setting up a development company but got stuck because, quite simply, as architects it wasn't allowed. People would make helpful comments like 'you'll have to resign as an architect'. Given that both of us had only just managed to become architects that didn't exactly appeal.

We began to wonder why we had spent years slogging away at college followed by the pain of the Part Three exam (the post-graduate professional qualification which is the final requirement towards formal registration as an architect). Our frustration was that, despite all these qualifications, it seemed we wouldn't be allowed to make a living through what seemed to be a very logical process of acting as both designer and developer for the projects we wanted to undertake.

Then magically the rule went. They didn't fudge it. They just scrapped it. So we immediately set ourselves up as architect/developers. I think we were probably the first in the UK to market ourselves as such. I don't think there was anything formal to be done other than quite openly say we are now architects and developers. A sort of coming out of the studio. Initially we set up a development company. Fairly quickly the business evolved into three separate parts, a design company, a development company and a construction company.

As far as our first project is concerned, I'm not sure how much of what I recall is the mythology that we wove around it and how much is reality. I was working in Glasgow at the time and getting the train backwards and forwards to my home in Edinburgh. Trains are always a good place to think and study. At that time they were rebuilding a tunnel on the direct route so the train took a detour. Going this long-way round meant that the journey time seemed interminable.

On occasion, not having anything better to do, I would read every page of the paper. And I mean every page – it's the only time in my life that I've actually read agricultural adverts. By my recollection it was in just such an obscure, hidden, bit of the newspaper that I discovered an advert. Edinburgh District Council was selling off some empty tenemental properties at West Crosscauseway/Buccleuch Street. This was alongside the adverts for cattle and sheep at the local mart.

I was surprised and intrigued by this very small, unprepossessing advert. It seemed quite out of proportion with what was actually being sold and quite frankly the Council could never really have expected anybody to respond to it. Later, when I spoke to David Beveridge who was then Head of Conservation at the Council, he said he had fought tooth and nail to bring it to the market with his Estates Department who had claimed nobody would wish to buy it. Estates felt that these properties should simply be knocked down. Perhaps it was an Estates Department ploy to appease David and his colleagues that they took out an advert. Presumably, when there was no response to this obscure advert, they could go back to the Committee with an impressive report saying 'I told you so'. If that was the ploy, it didn't work.

WEST CROSSCAUSEWAY / BUCCLEUCH STREET

The first stair to be sold was in West Crosscauseway: "We managed to arrange 100% mortgages for prospective purchasers. The queue for 12 apartments stretched from our temporary sales office in one of the apartments out into the street and snaked off round the corner – the first lot were sold in no time so we simply opened up the order book for the next three stairs and sold them on the same morning. And this was in an area which nobody thought would ever sell."

John Brown

"The Andys assembled a fantastic team of architects, technicians and quantity surveyors. Kenny Cooper, Stuart Davey, Alan Yeaman, John Gibson, David Miller, Damien Moore, Brian Maitland, Dougie Harley and our accountant Mary …, all crammed into three small rooms. Myself, Andy Doolan and an extremely talented young architect from Glasgow, Graeme Robertson, were squashed into a little room at the back which Andy Burrell christened 'The Creamery'."

Andy Bow

West Crosscauseway/Buccleuch Street, Edinburgh

We eventually paid £70,000. Again, it might be a trick of memory, but I'm pretty sure that everything we bought in the first few years cost £70,000. When you think about it £70,000 for something that eventually amounted to over 85 apartments wasn't a bad deal.

I did the appraisal. We were extremely naive but I cobbled together my best effort on our proposals. My appraisal for our first development ran to a full two pages.

In retrospect we were perhaps a little arrogant, as well as ignorant, but we felt we knew what Edinburgh needed. We had both been involved in housing issues, with a local Community Group, The Southside Association, in my case, with its newspaper, and Andy Doolan with its housing association. This was where we met and discovered that we had remarkably similar views.

We were both thoroughly fed up with bureaucratic jousting matches. We both felt we knew the area at grassroots and were impatient for change. There were stacks of empty buildings round about us in the south side of the city. We could empathise with students who were struggling to find places to live close to the University. We were aware that people had been shunted to the outskirts of the city, and, after their homes had been declared derelict, the buildings would sit empty for years and years. Redevelopment proposals had come and gone and the bureaucrats weren't doing enough to change things. Initiatives would come and go but progress was exceedingly slow – always two steps forward, one step back.

Andy Doolan and I had only arrived in Edinburgh in the mid 1970s. We took the city as we found it. We were certainly unaware of what the place had been like ten years previously when whole swathes of buildings on the South Side had been emptied. I had come to Edinburgh to study Planning in 1976 and so was aware that, in the late 1960s, the Council had adopted the Buchanan Plan recommending major new distributor roads running right through the South Side, Calton Hill and just about everywhere else in between.

A few years after the Council had approved the radical and destructive Buchanan recommendations, we started talking to them about scrapping these ideas. We weren't alone. Many local organisations were up in arms, particularly the Cockburn Association. The 1970s was a period of great change in Edinburgh's attitude at both the popular and civic levels. We were, I suppose, to arrive in the middle of all of that and play our part.

We took the debate to a further stage by simply asking the Council to give us a chance. Dump the idea of destroying so much of the fabric of the city and become more proactive and positive about restoring what was already there. We had worked as architects for other developers but most of those currently involved in the development business had their comfort zone, which was building new houses on largely greenfield sites. So when you came down to it the only option was to do it ourselves.

West Crosscauseway/Buccleuch Street consisted of eight tenement buildings varying in height from three to five storeys and including a number of small shops at ground floor level. One irony, which we thought was quite amusing at the time, was that included among these shops was the Southside Association's premises.

Despite the fact that we were actually doing things for the area the Association objected. They didn't like it, after all we had become nasty capitalists from the private sector and, in their eyes, turncoats doing things in a commercial way.

At that time the view of many was that social and environmental benefits should only be delivered by the public sector. If these tenements were to be improved then the work should be undertaken by a housing association – almost the post-war idea of providing "Homes for Heroes". Doolan and I were pragmatists and believed that there was plenty of scope in the south side for both housing associations and the private sector working alongside the local authority which, in those days, still counted house building as part of its remit.

Something else which amused us at the time was the fact that all our market assumptions were totally wrong. When we came to sell the apartments our sales strategy was based on a number of pretty simple notions. We were right in the middle of university land and next door to Edinburgh's largest hospital. So we thought these were ideal for daddy to buy a small apartment for "Samantha when she comes to the Uni". Or perhaps they would be starter homes for newly-fledged doctors and nurses arriving to work at the Royal Infirmary.

At the end of the piece, out of a development which ended up with 85 units, I think we sold three to people who were in some way, vaguely, connected to the University or the hospital. The rest went to an extraordinary mix of people, including quite a few who had been moved out of the area twenty years previously. They all desperately wanted to come back and live in the south side of Edinburgh and, until our development, they simply hadn't been given the opportunity.

This was a major lesson. The housing associations didn't regard somebody having lived there before as a key criterion to give them preferred status on their lists. The Council wasn't any better and here we were, all of a sudden, giving people the opportunity to move back into the area where they had been brought up or where they had lived before.

At that stage we used a £1 company through which we had made the initial application. As things moved on fairly rapidly we came to realise that our 'off-the-shelf' £1 company hadn't been properly set up as a development company so we had to move fast and reconstitute.

It was on another train journey to Edinburgh that I started to play around with the name. Again memory may be playing tricks but I seem to remember that I was actually travelling to a meeting with the Council. I rearranged the letters of our £1 'shelf' company and came up with the name Kantel on the grounds that this was pretty similar to the one we had acquired and it might be accepted as such. So from then on it was Kantel.

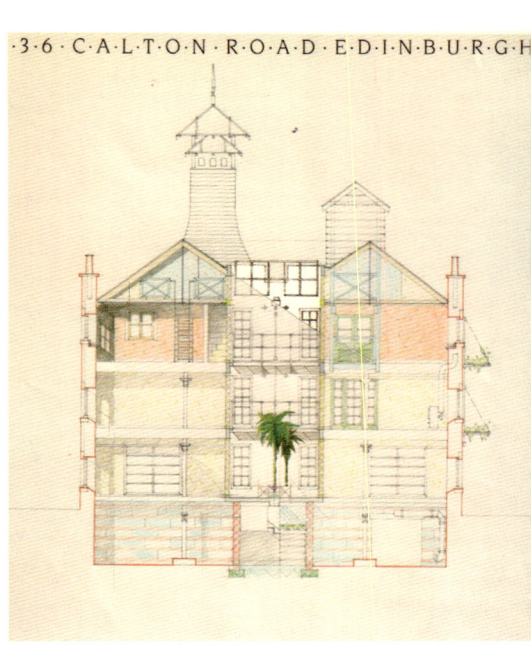

Calton Road Brewery, Edinburgh

CALTON ROAD BREWERY

"Rob came home one day absolutely fuming. Seemingly he'd been working on the cut-away drawing of the brewery which was later reproduced as the highly unusual brochure/poster for the development, and indeed framed by most of the inhabitants. The drawing was nearly finished on his drawing board and he quite happily went out for a quick lunch. When he came back the drawing had been embellished by Andy Doolan by the addition of a palm tree. Later, Rob would concede that the palm tree enhanced the overall effect but sadly, sitting next to Rob's drawing board, was one of his most precious glossy architectural books lying open at a picture of a fine building set in a verdant landscape but minus a distinctive palm tree which had been neatly removed by the aid of a pair of scissors. Rob went ballistic! It took a good wee while for him to get back on speaking terms with Mr Doolan."
Alison Wilson (formerly Hunter)

"The runt of the litter at Calton Road was a ground floor flat at the front. However the agents managed to shift it by employing the inspired selling line – 'Edinburgh's Worst Flat'. The Burrell Company's disarming honesty is so beguiling!".
Ian Moffett

I remember Doolan saying at the time how much he disliked the name. It had no ring to it, didn't mean anything and the first thing we would have to do, once we started trading, was to change it. So it's interesting that when Andy D. later acquired the name for a substantial sum he kept it going and it was still operating nearly a quarter of a century later. Like all these things you can dream up a name, any name, and once it gets used it starts to assume a level of credibility, a life of its own.

WITH OUR FIRST DEVELOPMENT we did the design work and led the construction process ourselves. It was the only way we could actually manage to make ends meet. Basically we had no assets, so the money we could borrow was minimal. It took us about three years to complete.

There is no question that that development influenced the way the Council was thinking. They had got shot of a pile of buildings which weren't the best they had to sell. They had even gained some cash in the process. The Council started looking at all the other buildings they owned which had been sitting around empty over the previous two decades. Most of them had been closed, on the premise that their accommodation was not up to current day standards. Their closure had been before the Housing Acts of the 1960s which encouraged renovation and the reuse of buildings rather than just knocking them down and starting afresh. For whatever reason they had been ignored and left to decay.

After our first endeavours the Council revisited its redundant housing stock. We'd proven that you could take an area and contribute to the regeneration process through property renovation. While the Planning Department had been very encouraging and worked alongside us, there were others within the Council who clearly had been very uncomfortable about the whole idea, and a few individuals within the Housing and Building Control Departments who were , at the least, unhelpful, and in some cases deliberately obstructive.

West Nicolson Street, Edinburgh

Forest Hill, Edinburgh

They seemed to be doing everything they could think of to thwart the process. The work we were doing was not, according to them, up to standard – we weren't doing things properly. It was a constant fight – day in, day out. But we knew that this was just politics with a small 'p'.

In those days you had to deal with people in Building Control who were more than happy to get the demolition men involved. In fact, we suspected that some of them had a rather closer relationship with the demolition companies than was truly healthy. Or maybe they just liked watching things being knocked down. So while quite a few local councillors were being very supportive, there were officials who made it quite clear that they didn't want us around. Somehow we survived and, through time, quite a few of those who had made things difficult didn't.

THERE FOLLOWED A FLURRY of abandoned buildings being marketed by the Council. We didn't get them all but we did get a few. Our next project was West Nicolson Street. The interesting thing about that development was that, in response to political concerns, it was determined that those properties should be for rent, not for sale to owner-occupiers.

With West Nicolson Street we agreed that it didn't have to be the developers who rented out the properties. So long as they were sold on to somebody who would rent them for a number of years that would be acceptable to the Council. I can't remember whether it was ten or twenty years. The strange irony was that these properties had been closed down in the late 1950s or early 60s largely to allow for the expansion of the University. At the end of the piece the University had never expanded. In the 1970s they realised that the planned expansion of the University wasn't needed, that the population was not going to grow exponentially, and that the University needn't occupy huge swathes of south Edinburgh beyond its existing campus.

The University had encouraged the Council to evacuate these buildings and now they didn't need them. The Council was stuck and didn't quite know what to do. So they sold them to us. We restored and converted them to student residencies and then we sold them to the University. The University rented them out and apparently they were hugely popular right from the word go. This was just another of these strange circular patterns. Buildings which were to have been demolished for the University were now being occupied by the University. They are still in University use and, hopefully, still popular with students.

When work on our first development at West Crosscauseway was still ongoing the Government had the inspired idea of encouraging renovation by allowing Improvement Grants to be sought by developers and not just owner occupiers. Overall we probably got support for about five or six projects but one I particularly remember was at Forrest Hill, behind the famous Sandy Bell's Bar. By this time we had developed a relationship with the Estates people at the University. They owned some of this group of derelict buildings, part of a former poorhouse, which were being squatted in and vandalised, including the odd bit of fire-raising. The University's problem was they didn't own all of the apartments. Nevertheless we agreed to buy their apartments from them.

Our inspired lawyer, Ian Moffett, then of Dundas & Wilson, had noticed that many of the empty flats which were privately owned belonged to people with names which sounded as if they might be Polish in origin. Certainly there was a profusion of 'z's and 'k's in the names. It was a long shot but he went to Edinburgh's only Polish law practice and suggested that some of these people might be their clients. His inspiration proved right, and after contact was made with these individuals – who must have expected a statutory repair notice – with the good news that a crazy development company actually wanted to buy their apartments, we were able to secure ownership of virtually all of the building.

Eventually the Forresthill building gave us 28 units. When we put them on the market there were people queuing down the street to buy them in what had been another little area of Edinburgh that most people had forgotten about. The fact that they overlooked Greyfriars churchyard meant that they were in a spectacular position with long views to the city beyond. We felt that, once again, we'd helped in a small way to change the patterns of development in the city and we were making progress.

THE NEXT CHAPTER WAS a bit of a departure. Calton Road was the first time that we had taken on an obsolete industrial building rather than something which had previously been residential. This building had initially been a brewery and most recently had been in use as a tyre depot. We acquired it in order to convert to purely residential use. This was a new sort of challenge. The brewery was on a difficult, north-facing, sloping site which rendered parts of the building dark and difficult to inhabit. We drove a lightwell down through the centre of the building and split the warehouse in a cruciform pattern around this source of light and air. We also employed the cramped, unlit, ground floor for car parking.

Unfortunately the challenge brought out the worst tendencies in us as architect/developers. The building was architected to the n'th degree and ended up looking brilliant, working very well - and losing us a lot of money! However it was a superb scheme and it probably gained us more gongs and awards than everything up to that time put together.

ANOTHER BIG CHALLENGE for Kantel was Castle Terrace. What had been residential apartments but had eventually been converted into a nurses' home and then offices for a health board. They were trying to sell it as offices but it really didn't work as such. It was just a relentless series of rooms banging through from one gable wall to the next. The building was a mess of long corridors and unpleasant office space.

Unfortunately, because these things are never easy, some of the offices in the building were still occupied on leases which couldn't be terminated. I remember that we found a nursing association and the office for the Scotland's

Castle Terrace, Edinburgh

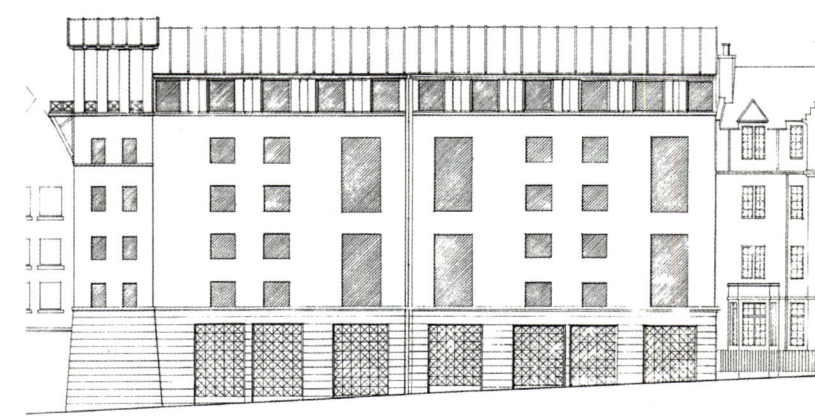

West Port, Edinburgh proposal

Garden scheme in the middle floors. We grouped them into a section of the building where they had access off the street and that allowed work to begin on the remainder.

We had a Japanese architect working with us at the time – Eisaku Ushida, eventually of Ushida Findlay, whose Scottish wife, Kathryn, I had known from our schooldays. He drew the elevation. Unfortunately for us he didn't draw it exactly as it was but took it upon himself to draw back in a chimney which nicely balanced the elevation of the building. By that time the chimney was long gone, presumably removed as a danger many years before. Our misfortune was that Historic Scotland admired the drawing and thought that replacing the chimney would be great. They imposed this as a condition. Therefore we had to add a massive stone chimney of incredibly intricate design.

Initially we looked for alternative ways of constructing it. Perhaps a cast facsimile would be good enough. In fact, as it turned out, rebuilding in natural stone was only going to be about ten percent dearer than doing the whole thing in concrete and fake stone because of the complexity of the structure. Happily, Historic Scotland coughed up a significant sum towards the work. I still look up whenever I pass by and reflect on the single, bright, beautiful chimney stack and the other which looks a bit more worn and, in appropriately Japanese fashion, mutter a blessing on Mr Ushida.

After Castle Terrace, Edinburgh became a bit problematic. There had been a change in the make up of the Council and they seemed hell-bent on attacking nasty profiteering developers who, they claimed, were exploiting government grants.

The newspapers took up the cudgels on their behalf. It probably wasn't intentional, just incompetent, that various reports appeared in local papers stating that developers were getting seventy-five percent of the cost of improving buildings. It simply wasn't true – in fact the grant eligibility rules meant that grant support was limited to something like £3,000 or £4,000 per unit.

The irony was that ninety percent of grant monies actually came from the Scottish Office, from national budgets, so the gain for Edinburgh was considerable. It cost the City very little indeed. As the Council owned most of the empty property in Edinburgh which, until this time, simply couldn't be improved, partially because the costs didn't stack up, it was even more ironic that the Council decided to throttle the goose that had been laying the proverbial golden egg.

We weren't the only developers who suffered from this absurd situation. However, one very senior Councillor in his wisdom, decided that we should be a particular target for his venom. Maybe it's because our offices were close to the Council Chambers and the pubs that some of the councillors frequented. He publicly berated the company and accused us of being all manner of rip-off merchants. In response we thought 'stuff you, we'll go elsewhere'. So we turned to Glasgow.

INGRAM SQUARE WAS FAR BIGGER than the Edinburgh projects that we had worked on. Glasgow had a Council which wanted to get things done, and the Scottish Development Agency had been given a specific remit by the Scottish Office to promote urban regeneration. Happily for us the Merchant City was the area they wanted to start with. Ours wasn't the first scheme in the area but it was by far the largest. In fact, it was probably the first inner city regeneration project of that era in Scotland which focused on a whole street block rather than a single building or a small group of buildings.

We had begun to realise that we couldn't do all the design work ourselves to the standard that we wanted to achieve. Unfortunately what we had initially set up had become a bit of a sausage machine. The demands of the machine were that we had constantly to find new projects in order to keep everybody employed. This wasn't a good way to run a business.

So the shift of attention to Glasgow coincided with the realisation that we were unlikely to prosper if we kept operating in the same manner. Ingram Square would

be undertaken by Kantel as developers, not as a multi-disciplinary team. That's when we took on Elder & Cannon Architects, who in those days were a young, go-ahead company. Not that they haven't remained pretty dynamic but, oddly, the founding partners seem to have aged at just about the same rate as the rest of us.

BUSINESS PARTNERSHIPS ARE NOT always easy. Andy Doolan and I both had our own ways of doing things and were pretty determined to progress things according to our separate priorities. Initially, as we drifted apart, we considered a geographic split. My suggestion was that Andy D. should concentrate on Glasgow and I would be responsible for Edinburgh and try to build things up that way. However, probably with some justification, Andy D. was concerned that the huge ambition of the Glasgow project might never be achieved or that business might not grow from there. The geographic split would also mean that we would have to rely on each other to make decisions on behalf of the company. Given the scale of operations it rapidly became apparent that the arrangement would be unworkable as we had quite different views on how things should be done.

The ultimate agreement to split wasn't particularly acrimonious but, perhaps naively, we hadn't really taken into account how everyone we worked with, and particularly the banks, would react. When we indicated our intentions, the banks were quite unequivocal in their view that we shouldn't do it, they didn't want it and we shouldn't even think about it (until they got their money back!).

Having to stick together when you've come to the natural end of a partnership doesn't sound like the best business plan. However, for Ingram Square in particular, we had an established joint venture (including Glasgow City Council and the Scottish Development Agency) and a partnership which the banks were comfortable with. So we had to follow the same course until the project was completed. Otherwise we divvied up everything. Andy took some projects, I took

some projects and, apart from Ingram Square, we went our separate ways.

Ingram Square was the last project undertaken by the original Kantel. The company had achieved quite a lot in five years and, I reckon, helped change the development scene in both Edinburgh and Glasgow. West Crosscauseway was truly pioneering and the Edinburgh projects which followed, West Nicolson Street, Forrest Hill, Calton Road and Castle Terrace were significant achievements among many restoration projects which provided new homes in the heart of Scotland's capital.

Of course the splitting up of Kantel wasn't easy. Predictably there was a period of waiting until the whole thing had been agreed in all its legal complexity. We didn't really want to proceed with new initiatives until it was quite clear that there would be no problems with ownership of new work. This was despite the fact that our new work was being brought in by a wholly new organisation. We simply couldn't power ahead before the old organisation had been fully laid to rest.

One key character in this narrative, who should have been credited before, is Rob Hunter. Rob had been involved at Calton Road as lead architect in our in-house team. His influence on that design was crucial as indeed it was on many other projects. Then, when Andy Doolan and I came to split the company, Rob and Peter Taylor who had been involved on the financial and administrative side of things went off with one of the contracts team to do their own thing. Sadly for them it didn't work out and the venture was pretty short lived. Thereafter Rob settled back into pure architecture which made the best use of his extraordinary talent.

AS THE BURRELL COMPANY EMERGED from the dissolution of the original partnership, I was joined by Raymond Ross, as our Financial Director, and by John Forbes who had been working with Nicholas Groves-Raines Architects. John was another architect with a strong predilection for development. He had been working on the development side of Nick's

business and had decided that this was the type of work he wanted to concentrate upon.

We set out to grow the Company again, John to pursue new opportunities and Raymond to ensure that the financial side of the business was kept tight.

We were now in the mid 1980s. As Ingram Square ran on we were starting to do things as The Burrell Company. West Port, Robertson's Close and Old Assembly Close on the High Street all got underway about this time.

There were some notable successes in the early stages. We acquired the assets of an English company which had made a foray into Scotland and then decided to go back south. Included in their portfolio was Carrick Quay. We picked Balfour Beatty Homes as our development partners for that one. My reasoning was pretty simple. Balfour Beatty were used to building apartments and, as the scale of the development was a little beyond us, we certainly needed a well-established development partner. As it turned out, it was a bit more than that division of Balfour Beatty had coped with before, not least because the design, by Davis Duncan Architects, was pretty innovative for the time.

As things turned out, Carrick Quay cost a lot more than it should have done. We would probably have come out of this one okay had the conclusion of this, our first major development in Glasgow under The Burrell Company heading, not coincided with the end of the 1980s and the recession starting to bite. In fact as we moved towards that particularly difficult time we were probably doing a little too well for our own good.

AT THE START OF 1987 we became only the second company in Scotland to seek funds through the Business Expansion Scheme (BES). This had been established by the government as a mechanism for raising project finance through a sort of limited share release. The process raised close to £2m. However, the trouble with this sort of programme is that it costs a great deal to set up so, while

Ingram Square, Glasgow

CARRICK QUAY

"The challenge was to produce modern riverside housing. We decided to create a rhythm of large repeated tenemental blocks with a strong nautical resonance. To demonstrate the principle we produced a very careful model of a single bay which became part of our submission for the competition – which, happily, we won!"
Ray Davis

"In our early years the relationship with Kantel and then The Burrell Company was always amicable but typified by one-way traffic. I described our practice as a 'finishing school' for Burrell Company architects".
**Nicholas Groves-Raines,
Groves-Raines Architects**

Carrick Quay, Glasgow

Old Assembly Close, Edinburgh

you might raise a substantial sum, a large percentage of that disappears in charges.

The BES company was set up quite separately from our main development division. We'd established our BES because the banks at that stage tended only to fund seventy or eighty percent of a project. There was therefore a deficit which had to be met from elsewhere and the BES mechanism seemed to be a good way of bridging that gap. So the BES company would invest in projects introduced either by Burrell or by others which were regarded as a good risk in return for a significant proportion of the development return.

As the 1980s progressed the banks built up the level of their contributions until they were 90% or even one hundred percent funders of some projects. Of course when the recession hit they found themselves in a position where they could take control of companies without any additional outlay. Then they would ditch the existing directors and install their own team, proceed with the development and take all the profit. Rumour has it that through the recession of the early 1990s one of Scotland's clearing banks became the biggest property company north of the border.

ONE OF OUR EDINBURGH JOBS around that time, Old Assembly Close on the High Street, is interesting because, although the first phase was completed in the 1980s, we revisited the area fifteen years later. Old Assembly Close provided a mix of residential and offices and was ultimately linked into a whole series of developments under our Buredi banner at Parliament Square, the Tron and the Wireworks (which in turn opened up the former nursery school site on the Cowgate for re-use).

At around the time that we were working on Old Assembly Close we were approached by the Faculty of Advocates who needed office space. If we would let them have the Wireworks building the Advocates would give us parking space at the rear of that property. The building was only really suited to office use.

Ultimately the proposed deal with the Faculty didn't come off. We found them impossible to work with. Frankly in almost three decades working in the property business, I've never dealt with such slippery characters. One committee after another wouldn't conclude, wouldn't agree to anything, dragged out the process and, not surprisingly, it was difficult to find anybody to represent us legally. What an example!

With Old Assembly Close we decided that, as well as retaining commercial uses on the ground and first floors (this was, after all, where the Edinburgh Festival Fringe was based), we would put in two- and three-bedroomed apartments above. We felt that as the Old Town's population had declined to less than 3,000, there might be a need for larger apartments to bring in families and at least start the process of reoccupation. The apartments sold straight away. It proved the point that it wasn't only students who wanted to live in the Old Town.

This was one of a number of turning points which changed people's attitude to the Old Town generally. Gradually over the last two decades the area has changed out of all recognition. Over the years, work on the streetscape, on reducing traffic volumes and on improving retail provision has made a huge difference to the Old Town and, in fact, to many people's perception of Edinburgh itself.

MORRISON STREET WAS OUR NEXT major challenge. We were approached by the property company Argent who were keen on exploring the development potential of the old good's yards at Haymarket. They wanted someone with local knowledge who shared their design aspirations for the site and who would ultimately undertake the residential aspect of the development while they concentrated on the commercial.

Morrison Street was one of those unfortunate cases where officials in the Council make the running and operate to their own agenda. The land was Council-owned so, when they were approached by Argent and ourselves, they bombed out our initiative and decided to run their own

competition. Perhaps they felt uncomfortable operating with just one development group on such a large site but the fact that we had made the running should, arguably, have given us some advantage. No matter, they decided to proceed with another competition.

Argent had brought Ted Cullinan on board as their architect. We were delighted. Unfortunately the Council officials determined that Cullinan's scheme for the site, which we had all expended huge time and effort over, should not be short-listed. Working with Argent we had done our homework and because we had been working on it for two or three years we were way ahead on all aspects – commercial, technical and design.

So ultimately when we didn't even make it to the last three and there was no cogent explanation offered, we were all somewhat surprised and just a little bit hacked off. Instead, alerted to the prominence and importance of the Morrison Street site, the Council had short-listed three schemes, none of which, in my view, was of any great architectural merit. This was quite contrary to the Council's insistence that design should be a key determining factor. The whole debacle was a major missed opportunity for Edinburgh.

Ted's scheme wasn't the only good one that had been rejected. My former business partner, Andy Doolan, had worked with Piers Gough on a scheme but this too was rejected. The Morrison Street competition was won by a local team but then the recession kicked in, the scheme was abandoned, and the recriminations began. It was clear that the Council had missed a great opportunity and ignored the depth and quality of the options available to them. In a rather 'tongue in cheek' sort of way we organised an exhibition to show what might have been – our very own 'Salon des Refuses'. The exhibition proved to be more popular than the rival Council one, and received more television and press publicity.

The great regret with Morrison Street was that here was a chance to take a large chunk of Edinburgh and masterplan it. Instead it was reduced to a piece-meal carve up into different

"We were first approached by The Burrell Company for a 'chat' about the Robertson's Close job. Andy was very keen that we should work speculatively. Predictably, I was less keen so I proposed that we should split the speculation 50:50. I knew what the usual developer response would be to such a suggestion. However, Mr Burrell's response to my request that we would put in £10,000 worth of work if he put in £5,000 worth of money was firstly laughter and then, surprisingly, agreement. It was the start of a beautiful friendship."

"When I got the invitation from Andy Burrell to meet him and Peter Taylor for lunch in a posh Edinburgh restaurant to discuss the Robertson's Close job I really felt that we'd made it. Here was me, a partner in a wee Glasgow practice, dining out in grand style. However, my perspective changed slightly when, at the end of a very boozy, very good lunch, Messrs Burrell and Taylor were unable to come up with either cash or a credit card between them. So for their treat I picked up the tab. Perhaps it was some sort of Edinburgh test."

"John Forbes had produced some initial schematics to describe the massing of the building and how it might fit on the corner. We jazzed it up in a post-modern idiom, adding the feature corner and spiral stair to enliven the block."
Ray Davis

sites and it was all a bit of a hash. Fifteen years later only half of it has been developed. The other half is still a car park.

ONE CHRISTMAS TOWARDS THE END of the 1980s, Santa brought a book on Scottish landscapes. One designed landscape which the book considered in some detail was the park of Duddingston House. A couple of months later I was out driving and the thought struck me that I didn't know how much of the original Duddingston parkland still existed, so I drove up the long driveway and was astonished to see that not only was the landscape there, albeit converted to a golf course, but the house itself was still standing.

The house at that time was functioning as an hotel. People would arrive at the front door of this grand building, imagining that they had really struck lucky, then would be shown through a side door into a room in a converted Nissen hut. These had survived from World War II when the place had been a Polish army camp. It was in a time warp.

When I arrived at this strange set-up, it was the end of February and their Christmas tree was still up. I thought then that business might not be too brisk. We started talking to the owners to see if they would be prepared to sell and eventually we came to an agreement.

The buildings are Grade 'A' Listed. After the war it seems they had been left empty and been vandalised. In the 1950s there was talk of demolishing them. By the early 60s the site was fortuitously bought by the builder/hotelier who saved the main building. He had restored the house but the stables and servants' quarters were in complete disrepair. He had also carried out a not terribly successful conversion of the original laundry into three apartments.

Our original aspiration was to perpetuate Duddingston House's use as an hotel – but a radically different one! We really wanted to produce something very grand and special – a real country house hotel. We had reviewed various other ideas, including some sort of use in tandem with the surrounding golf club but they showed no interest. We found an hotelier who wanted it as part of a chain of country house

"Burrell was in the vanguard of the conservation movement. Many of Scotland's best architects started out on conservation and if there was one developer which really helped in that process, it was Burrell!".
Malcolm Fraser, Malcolm Fraser Architects

"Arriving just as the recession was kicking off in 1988, wasn't perhaps the best timing. The period that followed, particularly our problems with Lilley going down, was certainly challenging. We pared the office to a minimum, effectively Andy, John and myself with a part-time secretary and sub-let most of the building. The task was to keep going. Gradually things improved."
Raymond Ross

"Rob's designs sold well because he managed to create very contemporary but nevertheless very welcoming spaces. It's interesting to note twenty years on that these apartments still feel unusual, very contemporary but very pleasant to live in."
Alison Wilson (formerly Hunter)

"The Burrell Company's commitment to giving good established architects, and more importantly emerging talent, a chance has been a continuous theme through everything they have done. They also understand that you can actually have a debate about architecture".
Gordon Murray, GM+AD

Morrison Street, Edinburgh

Duddingston House, Edinburgh

"The financial challenge of the development process is that every new project is just like starting up a new company. The fiscal, administrative and legislative problems are always different and The Burrell Company has never shied away from mixed-use developments which simply add to the complexity."
Raymond Ross

"The great transition in the way the Burrell Company operated was, I think, their decision to employ outside architects. From then on some of the best design talent in the country was producing some of the best housing Scotland has ever seen within a superbly innovative development model".
Nicholas Groves-Raines, Groves-Raines Architects

"Over the years I have worked with the Burrell Company on several occasions and visited often. One major attraction is that their highly efficient office seems to run on pure distilled humour – virtually unique in my experience".

"A benefit of working with developers who are also architects is that it cuts down on the need to explain. Instead the Burrell style seems to be about judicious criticism and proper support".
Piers Gough, CZWG

hotels. It took a while but I began to realise that everybody thinks country house hotels are a great idea but they don't usually make much financial sense, and getting somebody to invest seriously is very difficult. Once again the recession thwarted our ambitions. The hotelier backed off and we were left with the building.

We were beginning to run out of ideas and still hadn't found a single user. We approached Historic Scotland and the Royal Commission on the Ancient and Historical Monuments of Scotland. Both organisations were looking for new office locations. Historic Scotland was based at Dundas Street and we thought Duddingston House would have been ideal. Alas they decided they didn't want to be in the south of Edinburgh. Ironically they eventually moved into Longmore House in Newington, itself in the south of the city. It seemed a pity, that, rather than move into an A Listed magnificent manor house, Historic Scotland opted for a pretty mediocre, run of the mill, former hospital. The RCAHMS did even worse – also to the South Side of the city.

The only apparent option left with Duddingston House was to sell it to a developer who had approached us and who wanted to redevelop the property as housing. We agreed to sell. However once started, and having put in quite a lot of work, they ran into financial difficulty so the property reverted to us.

Eventually we decided that the main house should be restored for office use. It would have been daft to try and split it up. We then had the task of converting the wings of the house which we ultimately converted into three units each. It wasn't a successful project for us even though it is undoubtedly an achievement to save such important buildings from possible ruin. With greater resources we could have retained more of the original fabric. In retrospect the recession was not a good time for such an undertaking. Ten years earlier or later it could have been a quite different story but sometimes the opportunity comes about at the wrong moment and you've just got to make the best of it.

FETTES VILLAGE

"The design of this scheme was inherited from the retirement housing specialists Macarthy and Stone. One virtue of what we took over was that this was among the first condominium-style developments in Scotland with internal pedestrian streets. Unfortunately, the planners were not for radical change to the designs so we had to manage as best as we could with some judicious tinkering."
Ray Davis

Fettes Village, Edinburgh

Tollcross, Edinburgh

Crown Street, Gorbals, Glasgow submission

FETTES VILLAGE WAS A CHALLENGE of quite a different type and on a much grander scale than Duddingston. The house builder, McCarthy and Stone, had decided that Edinburgh was ready for a retirement village of around 350 units. This was a pretty bold importation of an American concept.

After they started building and realised just how little interest there was in Edinburgh for this idea they decided to sell the development on. We bought the site complete with some of McCarthy & Stone's construction work. It was a great site. One of the best in Edinburgh.

As with other large projects we didn't have the cash to go it alone at Fettes. The Earl Grey Street site at Tollcross was another area which we owned a big chunk of. With my characteristic aplomb at choosing joint venture partners, I had selected Lilleys (a blue-chip stockmarket listed company) for both sites who then went bust on us, so we were left 'holding the baby'. And it was a pretty big and pretty demanding baby at that.

We didn't own all of the Tollcross site. One big chunk of it was owned by the Council but we had done a deal with them so that we could take on the keycorner site at Tollcross and give them some land they wanted elsewhere. Our architect, Campbell & Arnott, produced a very interesting, high-density scheme.

Unfortunately, as is often the case with these things, this development got absolutely bogged down in the stupidity of car parking. It seemed absurd that the number of car parking spaces should dictate what was to happen on a key city centre site. We had suggested that we should build a car park to provide office parking during the day followed by residential parking in the evening. Thus if you owned one of the flats you would have dedicated car parking but you wouldn't have full ownership of a specified parking space. We even had the complex management system drawn up. The Council insisted on a Section 75 arrangement (a tortuous legal agreement which attaches to the title of the property) so we spent the next two years trying to cajole their legal

department into an agreement to produce a written document. Meanwhile we couldn't do a thing on the site.

We had a contract to build student housing in place when the receiver was called into Lilleys. The bank thought that they could assume ownership of the Tollcross site lock, stock and barrel. However, with our various agreements we were set to control a major central Edinburgh site for a net debt of approximately £300,000. In bankrupting Lilley the bank broke these agreements and everything fell apart. I remember Raymond trying to convince the bank that they would be much better off retaining the stand-alone company that owned the site but their response was to stop taking notes and, presumably, blame it all on Lilleys or someone else, but certainly not themselves. Ultimately the bank had to meet an acquisition cost of several million pounds. Happily we were long gone by that stage and had moved on to other things.

All we had achieved at Tollcross was to spend time and money – and then the recession hit. Maybe in the circumstances it was fortuitous that we hadn't managed to actually start on site and incur major expenditure. Who knows?

The timing of our Edinburgh ventures with Lilley were hugely unfortunate. What should have been two very good schemes were thwarted by three and a half years of recession and, without the strength of a larger company to help us ride it out, it was always going to be difficult.

However, we survived the recession. It had taken us twelve years to grow and three years to shrink, a recurring pattern in our industry. Inevitably, in times of recession, the banks don't want to lend on speculative development. We didn't have major assets to borrow against so, in order to keep going, we had to diversify.

In the early 1990s we retrenched. In retrospect the wise thing to do would have been to get out of Scotland, and seek opportunities south of the border. It wasn't until much too late that we realised that Scotland's politicians were reacting to the recession quite differently from the rest of the country. With our track record we would have been well

"Our pitch, with Burrell, for the first phase of Crown Street followed the masterplan with, we all hoped, real innovation and flair. We were perhaps just too much ahead of our time".

"We all thought that our masterplan for Laurieston which followed the success of CZWG's winning design for Crown Street would be greeted with enthusiasm, or at least a modicum of gratitude. Instead the reaction indicated that the Council considered this too much of a presumption. So the potential for continuing the regeneration of Gorbals was thwarted".
Piers Gough, CZWG

"Over the years Andy Burrell and myself have worked together on some fantastic, major, ground-breaking projects. Unfortunately it's always been in the pub after work and nothing has ever come to fruition".

"Although our work is in the public sector, Molendinar Park and Burrell have a lot in common. Many of our respective projects have been similar in scale and for similarly difficult urban sites. We also share a similar taste in architects".
Rob Joiner, Molendinar Park Housing Association

"There is no question that the Burrell influence has spread throughout the UK. Although the development model they helped establish is now widespread, there is still nobody doing it better."

"The Burrell Company understands that good design sells. Their friends and disciples have carried that message far and wide".
Gordon Murray, GM+AD

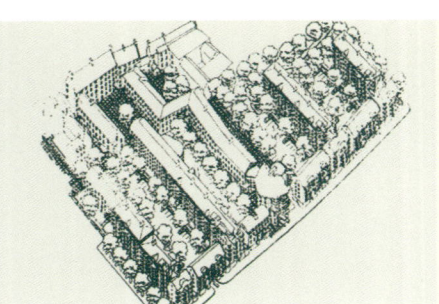

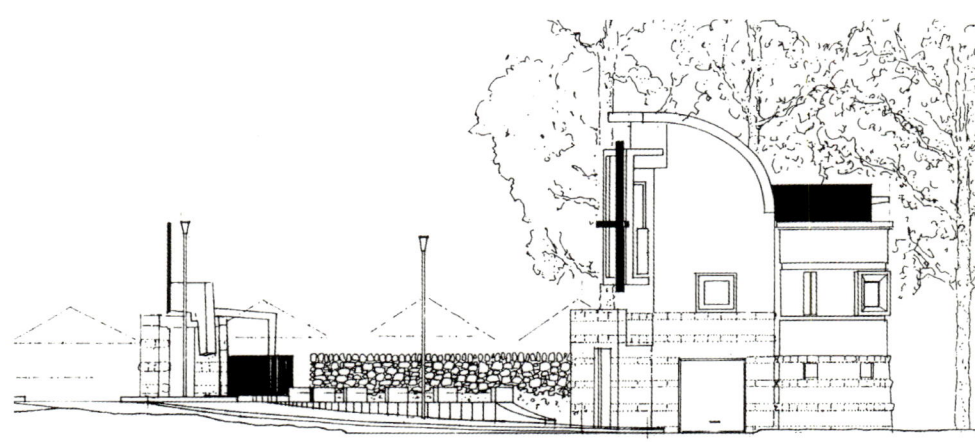

Woodside Terrace, Glasgow

Holyrood Brewery and Scottish Parliament

Fettes Lodge, Edinburgh

placed to take on work in Manchester, Leeds or Birmingham, all of which were being primed for major change. We would certainly have received financial assistance to help things move forward in a recessionary time. We had ventured south in the late 1980s but our reaction to recession was to retrench – a major missed opportunity and one I still regret.

What we tried to do at that time was to get our foot in the door in a manner which didn't present a high level of risk. Our idea was to work in partnership with other organisations in the hope that we could gradually bring in the cash.

We did a number of studies, looking at the potential of various sites. Among these was the Holyrood study which proposed splitting up the Holyrood Brewery site and moving it on as a series of projects. Our ideas were enthusiastically received and resulted in a tender process. Although we bid for a piece of the action we didn't get it. The same was true of our study of Glasgow's historic Briggait. We put forward a number of ideas but the City Council didn't take up any of them. In fact it was almost a decade later that the building would be brought back into use as artists' studios.

We did manage to keep going on smaller projects. We did a one-off office building in Woodside Terrace, Glasgow. There we tried to apply the techniques which we had developed and refined in house building to a speculative office development. It didn't work. So in the end we sold it on.

Another notable Glasgow speculation was at Candleriggs. Given the success of Ingram Square this proposal built on our apparently excellent relationship with the local authority. However, very rapidly it became clear that there were too many people involved, with too many agendas. Strangely the current approach to the Candleriggs area bears strong similarities to our mid 1990s proposals. The difference is that now the project is being promoted by the local authority rather than as a public private partnership.

GLASGOW WAS PARTICULARLY RICH TERRITORY for Burrell failures at this period. We entered the first development

competition for Crown Street, Gorbals. Piers Gough had won the competition to create the masterplan for the area so we worked with him to produce a brilliant proposal for the first building on the site which we felt should be a very positive statement of what was to come. Unfortunately the Crown Street Regeneration Project decided that, in time of recession, it was wise to err on the side of caution. So they went for a volume house builder and selected Millers, doubtless because they were fearful that a smaller company like ourselves might not deliver the goods.

It was a major cause of frustration at the time that the big house builders were being encouraged, both politically and financially, to create new housing and convert ex-council housing in the peripheral estates. While that may well have been necessary, the real need for urban regeneration in the city centres was ignored. This was where smaller companies like ourselves who understood the sort of innovative approaches that were required were certainly primed to help. However, the local enterprise companies, who should have been the vehicles for urban regeneration, were going through one of their phases of not supporting physical intervention so nothing was moving forward. Through most of the 1990s not a lot was happening on the Scottish urban regeneration scene. Certainly very, very little was in any way aided by the public agencies within any of Scotland's inner city cores. This contrasted with the experience in England.

Ironically the project that the whole local enterprise network points to, as far as urban regeneration is concerned, is Crown Street, Gorbals. It's generally acclaimed as a huge success. There is no doubt that it created a housing market in an area where there wasn't one before. Perhaps the very high cost to the public purse of galvanising the thing into action is justified. It certainly works well in terms of creating a masterplanned, mixed-tenure development of human scale in what previously had been a concrete hell. Personally I think they lost an opportunity of innovating in the architectural as well as the masterplanning approach. But then I would say that – they didn't choose us!

I suppose Crown Street exemplifies the Glasgow approach. The public money supporting the new-build there was much greater than, say, we had received for Ingram Square. I suppose it's a question of whether the local authority wanted partnership or to be in control. Glasgow, as a strong Council, want to run the show. As a local authority they have consistently taken the lead on projects. They want to design, masterplan and bring in developers to do what they want them to do. Of course they then have often had to give them large amounts of money to achieve this goal. It clearly works, but whether it's the most efficient use of resources is another question.

This whole period was characterised by grand ambitions and small projects. We took on a former boarding school at Napier Road, Edinburgh. We promoted it on the basis that if people bought in early we would work with them to custom design their homes. We also undertook a small project in the Dean Village.

The Fettes Lodge competition was more about reputation building and, on reflection, over this period we managed to maintain the illusion that we were still pretty major players when in fact the workload was quite piddling. Concentrating on small jobs allowed us the undoubted luxury of putting very substantial resources, way beyond what was sensible, into projects which fired us up. That included one or two projects where we were never going to make money but where we saw potential major benefit in the restoration of historic buildings or in upping the architectural ante.

THE NATIONAL PIPING CENTRE at McPhater Street, Glasgow was one where we were never going to make a return but which definitely gave us immense satisfaction. It was great to see a ruinous building coming back into use. As a centre it has certainly been of tremendous cultural benefit.

Years later in Manchester we were talking to some of their museums and galleries people. They were enthusing about the re-use of an historic building and the sort of commercial/cultural mix which would revitalise it. They referred to a

"Ramsay Garden was always going to be contentious, particularly considering the conservation issues for such a precious piece of Edinburgh's architectural heritage. However Andy Burrell met with the neighbours and spoke with such passion, knowledge and enthusiasm that they were all won over. The process was also helped along by the fact that one of the neighbours had an architect son who was well aware of The Burrell Company's track record on work on historic buildings and gave a glowing endorsement of their skills and sensitivity".
Ian Moffett

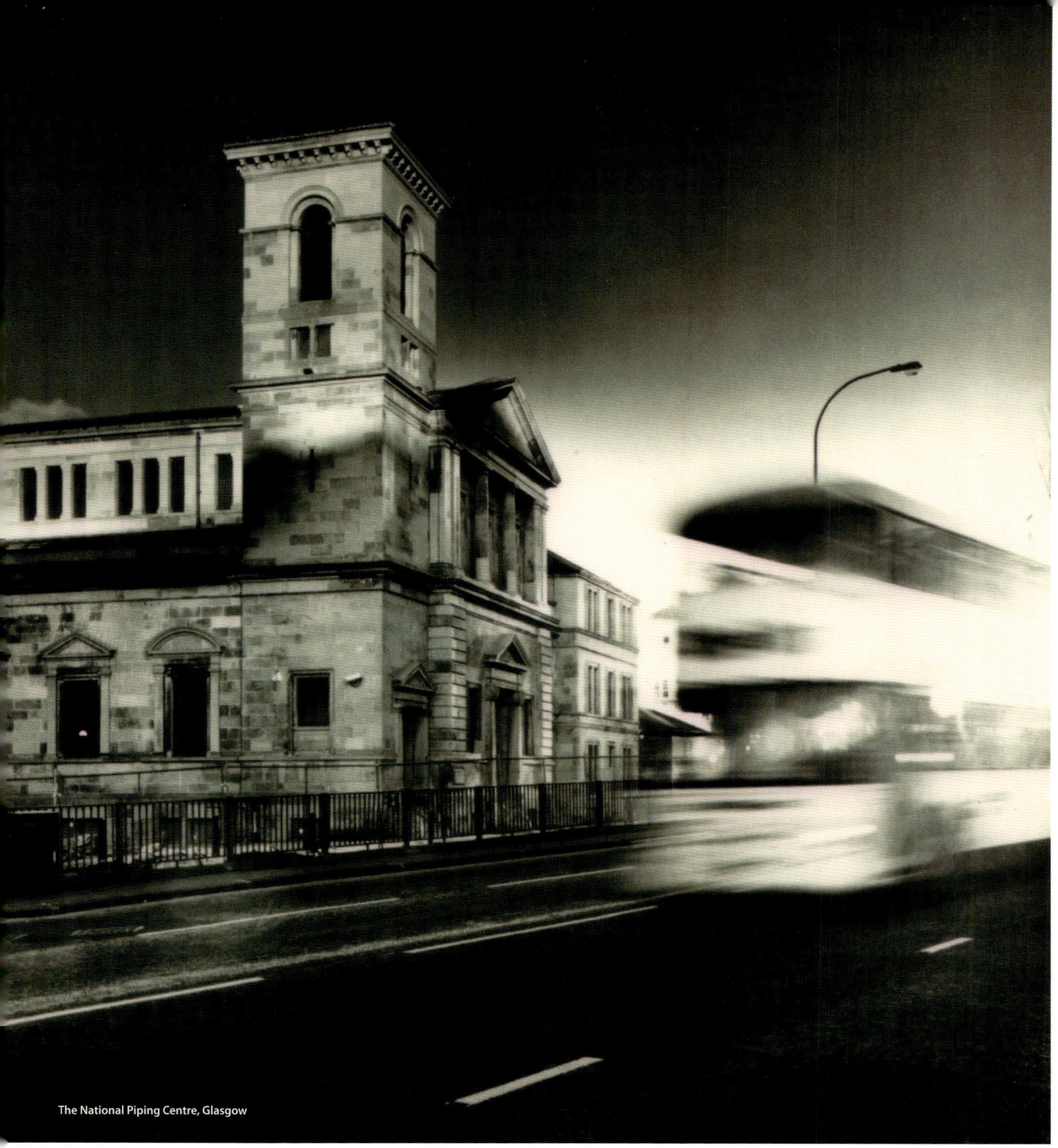

The National Piping Centre, Glasgow

"The National Piping Centre was extraordinarily complex and took us the best part of five years to complete. Andy Burrell was determined that it should be a worthy addition to the roster of national institutions. Not only is its architecture impeccably detailed but the whole thing is woven through with superb works of art".
Gerry Grams, City Design Advisor, Glasgow City Council

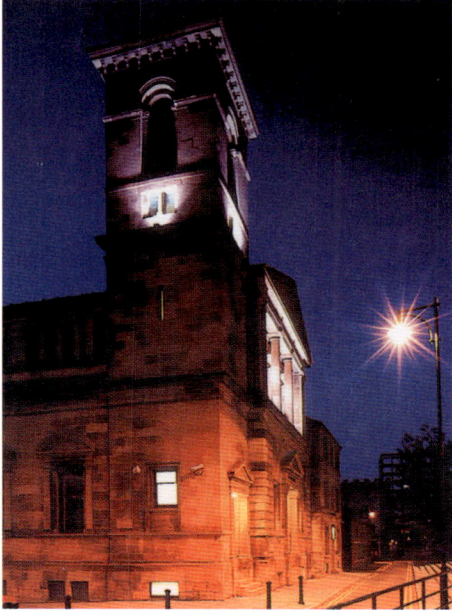

'superb project' in Glasgow which was exactly the sort of thing they envisaged for their property. The comment was, "You really must go to Glasgow and see the Piping Centre – that's exactly how it should be done!"

It's nice that, although people are unaware that you've been involved, they do consider it creditworthy. Of course, I made the point of modestly explaining the facts to our Manchester friends and have to say that their response, "Oh well you don't have to go and visit it then," was rather less than the enthusiastic praise I had been hoping for. But at least I saved the train fare.

ANOTHER GLASGOW PROJECT, on a slightly more grandiose scale, was the proposal to create a tower at St. Enoch Square. John Forbes and Stuart Gulliver, then Chief Executive of the Glasgow Development Agency, had been talking about iconic buildings and how to create an icon for Glasgow. The idea of a city centre viewing tower grew and developed from that chat. Unfortunately the chosen site was pretty awful but the international competition, promoted by ourselves and the GDA and administered by Neil Baxter, went brilliantly.

The winning design for the Glasgow Tower selected from a remarkable 353 entries by Stuart and a group of judges including such luminaries as Norman Foster, Anthony Hunt and David Mackay was very, very good. As time went on the tower was 're-located' to a new setting, beside Glasgow Science Centre on Pacific Quay. This site is much more prominent and gives the structure much greater visibility. It is a superb building – less successful as a work of kinetic engineering!

As we gradually emerged from recession the workload increased. Park School, on a hilltop site in the Park district of Glasgow, helped to kick-start the residential regeneration of what for years had been an office area. People argued that the area didn't have an established residential market and that we would have problems selling. In our view that was just daft. The area started as residential and had been inappropriately converted to offices. All we were doing was turning it back to residential.

Glasgow Tower Competition

Park School, Glasgow

When I went to visit Park School, with a view to redeveloping it as apartments, it was winter and therefore dark at an early hour. To this day my colleagues maintain that I failed to pick up the structural steelwork holding up the rear elevation. They use this against me as some sort of rationale for why it cost so much more than we had intended, which is probably true.

One nice thing about the Park development was seeing how many people who had been pupils at what was formerly a Glasgow girls school, come back to view what we had done. They reminisced about the art classes and the various rooms in which they had been students. Mind you, the key lesson I suppose I learned in this particular school experience was, don't survey in the dark!

Lots of people have converted properties back to residential use in the Park area since and Glasgow has benefited tremendously. In fact the residential boom in the area was such that we've never bought another building there – we simply couldn't afford to. The pace of residential change accelerated and the area is now a healthy mix of offices and residential which makes for a much more pleasant neighbourhood for all concerned.

DUBLIN COLONIES IN EDINBURGH was quite different in character from the grand terraces of Glasgow's Park area but no less significant as a ground-breaking development. This was our first link with EDI which would eventually lead to the formation of Buredi. EDI had been established as a wholly owned subsidiary of Edinburgh City Council. Its role was to promote development, sometimes on Council land, with the key aim of enhancing the city but also to generate revenue for the Council. Similar organisations had been established south of the border but this was the first in Scotland.

We knew the EDI people from their work in the Council. When Ian Wall left the Council to join Bill Ross at EDI one of his first tasks was the development of Dublin Colonies. EDI had agreed to acquire the site and promote its redevelopment through an architectural competition. By the time we came

on board this had all been done and they had chosen their scheme. The problem was it didn't work financially. Ian recommended to his Board that they should work with us on the basis that we knew about residential but always kept the quality of design to the fore – very much akin to his own views on how things should be done.

The deal was simple. If we could help them to make the project work and turn it into a viable development without compromising the quality of the overall winning scheme then we would develop the site as a joint venture. That's effectively what happened. Fortunately from our point of view John Forbes had studied with the architect of the development, Richard Murphy. Also, as architects, we were used to working with our fellow professionals and to adapting designs with appropriate compromises which weren't detrimental to the overall effect or the quality of the project.

Dublin Colonies reaffirmed our belief in partnership working on major developments. During the 1980s we'd worked with Lilley and Balfour Beatty but that tended to be on one-off projects. The relationship with EDI was destined to be different. After our first success with them we agreed that Burrell and EDI should set up a rolling joint venture company and seek other projects together.

THE NEXT BUREDI DEVELOPMENT after Dublin was Coalhill. This was a local authority site where Burrell had agreed that we would run a design competition and create something on the Water of Leith that would set a standard for the regeneration of the area. Until that point there had been quite a lot of poor-quality development, certainly not design-driven. Good sites were disappearing, built on by major house builders in the cheapest, meanest fashion that they could get away with. At Coalhill we were looking for something more iconic and felt that this project would fit nicely into the Buredi portfolio.

To up the ante we invited three architectural practices from Scotland and three from outwith to compete. The competition was won by one of the Scottish practices, Allan

Murray Architects. Our original idea had been to create a greater percentage of offices on the site than we eventually did but the market just wasn't going for it. The oval building had originally been intended as entirely office space, but we reworked it so that the two lower floors would be commercial with everything above residential. Thus both the oval and rectangular blocks were eventually mainly residential. At the end of the piece we got a distinctive development. It is also, undoubtedly, a benchmark for the area.

Another waterside site in Leith was Ronaldson's Wharf. For this one we worked with the Council on an architectural competition which was part of Edinburgh's bid for the City of Architecture prize. The Council asked us to help with preparing the brief and managing the process. As with the Glasgow Tower, we involved Neil Baxter to help in the delivery of the competition for this particularly sensitive site. Our judges were Henri Ciriani, John McAslan and George Kerevan. Even though Edinburgh lost out to Glasgow as City of Architecture, Ronaldson's Wharf was a success.

After we delivered the competition for the Council they gave us a watching brief so that the winning developer wouldn't just dump their successful scheme in favour of the usual banality. The project took a long time to come out of the ground. The winning architects, Dignan Reid & Dewar with Fraser Brown MacKenna, produced something of far higher quality than would ever have been achieved by simply selling the site without a development brief. It is an excellent scheme and the one tangible success of Edinburgh's 1999 City of Architecture and Design bidding process. Ronaldson's Wharf and Coalhill remain the most architecturally distinctive, contemporary developments in central Leith.

BACK IN THE HEART OF EDINBURGH we purchased what had been a Lloyds TSB management training centre. Ramsay Garden has to be the most prominent and picturesque development in the whole of Edinburgh. Our building was right at the heart of this extraordinary grouping of Arts and Crafts Victoriana, nestling just below the castle.

DUBLIN COLONIES

"This was our first job with Burrell. EDI had held a competition for small practices. Eventually our winning scheme was adopted by the new Burrell/EDI joint venture and set us on the road to a number of very positive collaborations."

Richard Murphy

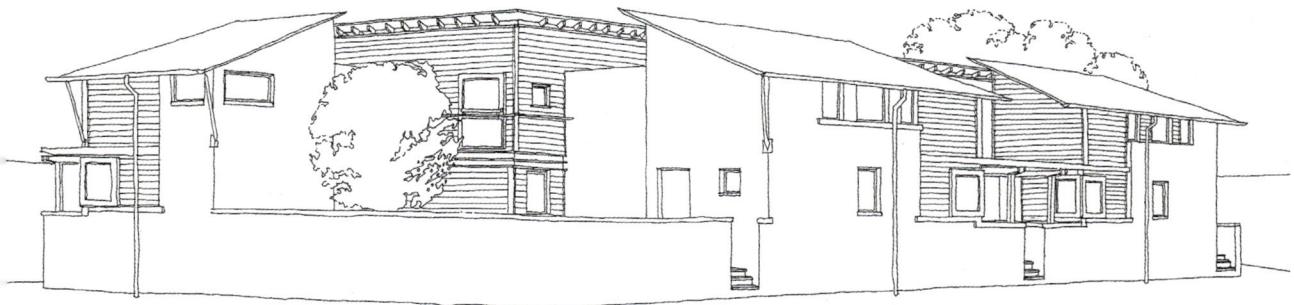

Dublin Colonies, Edinburgh

Ronaldson's Wharf, Leith, Edinburgh

Ramsay Garden, Edinburgh

When we first acquired the Ramsay Garden site we felt that this was a once in a lifetime opportunity. However it was a complete mess inside. The Patrick Geddes-inspired scheme incorporated the eighteenth century 'Goosepie House'. Over the decades it had been chopped, changed and generally botched around. When we started to strip it back we discovered that all sorts of mistakes had been made in the past, some of them with real safety implications, like floor joists which had been cut short of their wallhead..

Ramsay Garden looked great outside but we had a lot of internal rebuild on our hands. Its previous sub-division had been completely haphazard so, while we had a building which was amazing in parts, we realised that what we would be creating here would be very interesting apartments , not necessarily very good apartments. The form of the building just wouldn't allow us to create any really grand spaces.

To celebrate the completion of Ramsay Garden we were determined to hold a party. The coincidence of the impending annual Edinburgh Festival Fireworks Concert was too good a chance to miss. So we decided to hold a fireworks dinner. My major memory of the event is not of the delightful dinner, or the excellent company, but my trauma over how people decided to view the fireworks display.

The rear of the building was still obscured by our giant construction scaffold. We organised the dinner such that each of my colleagues hosted a table. Before the event, together with my fellow Directors, I ensured that everyone had an explicit brief. Whatever happened nobody was to go out onto the scaffold. There were two reasons for this. Firstly, there was no way our insurance would cover us for anybody falling off and, secondly, no matter how well built the scaffold might have been, it wasn't designed to hold two hundred guests.

As soon as the fireworks started many of our guests decided to completely ignore our advice and climb out onto the scaffold to get a better view. I even remember one of my colleagues, literally hanging off a scaffold pole, holding on with one hand whilst clutching a bottle of champagne in the other.

From my vantage point inside the building I witnessed all of this, sweating profusely. My mind raced over the legal implications of our sending a number of Edinburgh's great and good to their untimely demise, tumbling down the Castlerock. The legal implications were that bit more traumatic as, among our guests, were several Law Lords who, as I recall, were among the first to climb nimbly out through the windows to the construction platforms. I witnessed the most interminable firework display ever! Eventually it ended and they all climbed back indoors, I think all accounted for.

EARLY IN THE 1990s we started work on the remnants of a scheme which had been affected when Lilley went bust. We had been negotiating with the University of Edinburgh to acquire the site adjoining Tailors' Hall on Edinburgh's Cowgate. The University mistakenly assumed that, as our partners, in a totally separate, stand-alone, company, had gone bust, Burrell would follow. They took the proposed student housing deal and invited other developers to become involved.

We ended up with the booby prize – the difficult task of restoring Tailors' Hall itself. It was an A listed building which had been disused or certainly misused for the previous four decades. Within the grounds of the University, it was hidden behind a two storey high brick wall, preventing public access. It was partially used for University storage and partially derelict. Effectively we restored the exterior, made it structurally sound, and then sold it on for conversion into an hotel.

One interesting aspect of the whole Tailors' Hall experience was that we actually got an Historic Scotland grant to help with the work. They were concerned that such an important building should be restored to the highest possible specification so the whole process included very detailed and lengthy consultation with Historic Scotland.

Coalhill, Leith, Edinburgh

Tailors' Hall, Edinburgh

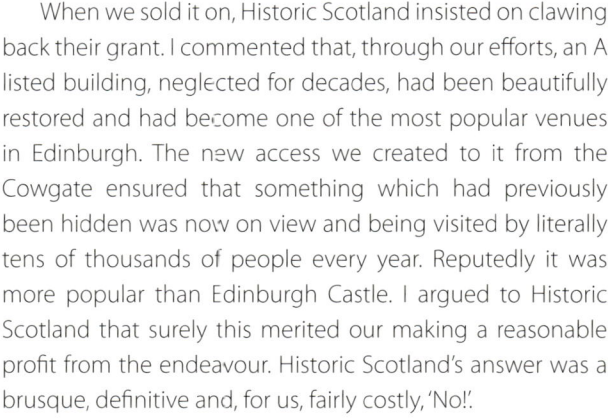

Bartholomew House, Edinburgh

Smyllum House, Lanark

"Our partnerships, with EDI, Premier and Places for People, broaden the range of what The Burrell Company can take on and the scale that it can handle at any particular time. They allow us to do what we do best, high-quality buildings which show the way forward for cities. While financing major projects is never going to be easy, the track record is fantastic and we are working with some of the best in the business."
Raymond Ross

When we sold it on, Historic Scotland insisted on clawing back their grant. I commented that, through our efforts, an A listed building, neglected for decades, had been beautifully restored and had become one of the most popular venues in Edinburgh. The new access we created to it from the Cowgate ensured that something which had previously been hidden was now on view and being visited by literally tens of thousands of people every year. Reputedly it was more popular than Edinburgh Castle. I argued to Historic Scotland that surely this merited our making a reasonable profit from the endeavour. Historic Scotland's answer was a brusque, definitive and, for us, fairly costly, 'No!'.

A much less contentious historic building which gave us a superb result, delighted the planners, won awards, generated eleven brilliant apartments and then became a complete marketing nightmare was Smyllum House near Lanark. What was originally a Strathclyde Building Preservation Trust scheme, but had proven unfundable or unachievable for whatever reason, had been offered to John Sheridan, who was working with us at the time. Behind the main facade the building had effectively fallen down. It was in total disrepair. Everything of merit had been removed and everything else comprehensively trashed.

We came up with a straightforward proposal to convert Smyllum into five units with six further houses set behind. It wasn't technically difficult to build and we worked on the presumption that eleven units in a fairly buoyant market wouldn't present too much of a problem. Unfortunately they were a bit expensive for Lanark at that time and it took ages to shift them. The press didn't help much because it transpired that the building had something of a past.

Seemingly Smyllum had once served as a children's home managed by a religious order. There were allegations of cruelty and these resurfaced when we were promoting our new development. While an ancient history of evil-doing might make for pretty positive marketing and the headless ghost adds undoubted cachet, the much more recent maltreatment of children gave our development a fairly

odd guilt-by-association. It seems pretty strange to blame the building but it made for a good press story, whilst we suffered.

OUR NEXT EDINBURGH PROJECT, Bartholomew House, had been sold on the open market. In retrospect we should have bought the whole site but we were still feeling bruised by the recession, so we took on the problematic and costly restoration of the historic building whilst a volume builder did the new-build.

The building, which had once been a famous map factory, had a rather portentous classical façade. The grand portico entrance came from a much older building which the Bartholomew family had owned. They had knocked down the rather grand Falcon House and, with typical Victorian thrift, had shifted the imposing bit up to the new factory. Behind the portico was a grand, domed entrance without much space on either side. There were, however, surviving original features in what had been the offices and we worked around these, using them as the focus of the various spaces.

Elsewhere in the building there was nothing of any merit, so these parts were designed in a contemporary manner. One of these apartments was sold to a graphic designer who was terribly keen on living there. It was a superb, double-height space which, when complete, looked very stylish indeed. A decade later we were surprised to see the same flat illustrated on a huge poster in Glasgow promoting a forthcoming loft development which would take lofts to a 'new dimension'. There were all sorts of ironies. This was an Edinburgh apartment, developed ten years previously, by ourselves, promoting futuristic loft spaces in Glasgow by someone else. We could only be amused, and a little flattered.

Bartholomew House was another of those instances where we invested a huge amount of time and effort towards a development which in the end only created a few units. We had come to the point that we really needed to work again on a larger scale.

Homes for the Future, Glasgow

THERE MAY BE SOMETHING OF a recurring theme in the fact that the opportunity to increase the scale came in Glasgow. Homes for the Future was part of Glasgow's City of Architecture and Design 1999 celebrations. To be honest when it was first launched we were fairly sceptical and imagined that they would be looking for a major house builder to do a variation of their standard thing. However, when we talked to the City of Architecture team it was quite apparent that they were seeking an exhibition piece. Because we had been involved with both the Glasgow and Edinburgh bids for City of Architecture and Design, we were keen on participating when Glasgow won it. As they really did want an exemplar project, we decided to really go for it. Looking back I still think it was a great idea.

Robert Burns said something about the best laid schemes of mice and men going horribly wrong. The concept of Glasgow City Council and the various supporting bodies acquiring the land, putting in the infrastructure, setting the design standards and then promoting the competition was all very good. Where it fell down was the programme because, although at the outset there seemed to be plenty of time to work things through, by the time the Council had actually acquired the land and Communities Scotland had indicated that some top-up finance would be available and the bureaucratic wheels had performed at their usual slow grind, we were left with a timetable that was completely unrealistic.

Time was far too short. In the normal course of things the programme would have been set back by the best part of a year. However 1999 was an immovable feast so we set to. Our big mistake was to agree to build on a management contract arrangement. The whole thing began to unravel fairly quickly.

Homes for the Future and, we like to think particularly our bits of it, is some of the best domestic architecture created in Scotland in the last twenty years. However, right at the death of the project and after the buildings were finished, we were stung by the contractor claiming massive additional costs.

In the end we spent more time in legal battles than we had been able to spend on the design process. We lost literally hundreds of thousands of pounds.

Homes for the Future may be another case of the more gongs you get the less money you make or in this case the more money you lose. Looking back it wasn't to do with the architecture, more the delays at the outset and the contractual arrangements that we were obliged to enter into in order to get the job done. In retrospect when we got to late 1998 and we still hadn't got the legals signed we should have chucked in the towel. We should have admitted that the buildings couldn't be procured in the time remaining. However there was an absurd and ill-founded optimism about the whole thing. We were sure we could do it if we managed it appropriately. Our theory was fundamentally flawed!

It took us a few years to get out of the legal wrangle which followed Homes for the Future. It still looks extremely good, in fact better now than it did at the time. The landscape has matured nicely and the residents in the Ushida Findlay building have done their own thing with the terraces. Thousands of people came to see the development in 1999 and it still ranks high on the international architectural visiting list. It was good for 1999, good for housing in Scotland and crippling for us. If you learn by your mistakes we were becoming pretty knowledgeable.

There is no question that the City of Glasgow learned something from the Homes for the Future experience and, since then, they have encouraged other housing providers to create developments of real merit.

WE THOUGHT WE'D FOLLOW UP Homes for the Future with a grand plan for 'New Laurieston' in Glasgow. It was a huge tract of land in the Gorbals and we wanted to encourage people to follow the model of Crown Street. Working with EDI and Miller we appointed Piers Gough who had done the Crown Street masterplan to create a proposal, based on the same principles, for Laurieston. We also intended to take on

the historic Laurieston House and other bits of important architecture which had fallen into dereliction in the area and use the new-build development to link the whole thing together.

It all seemed to us to be rather a good idea. We could work in tandem with the local authority and other private sector interests to make the whole thing work. We would get A listed buildings restored, advance the demolition of a couple of tower blocks that were scheduled to come down and create a really vibrant community on a massive swathe of land which had been underused since the 1960s and '70s clearance of the Gorbals.

Piers' masterplan for New Laurieston was very much low rise on the Maida Vale model. Effectively, the blocks enclosed gardens at the back which were protected and, in large parts communal, with the houses facing onto the street. It's certainly not rocket science, in fact bloody simple in theory. The skill comes in making it all work in architectural and urban terms.

Sadly our vision came to nothing. The City Council decided that this central area wasn't a priority. They would rather devote their energies and resources to other areas of the city. Whilst I don't have any argument or objection to the Council taking the lead where it has the resources, it seemed just plain daft not to allow the private sector to help regenerate the City. It's been over ten years since we submitted our New Laurieston scheme. In the interim precisely nothing has happened on the ground. The Piers Gough masterplan has been binned and I think there have been another two or three since. Laurieston House still languishes and the tower blocks, now very much past their sell-by-date, are still scheduled for demolition.

The New Laurieston story puts me in mind of one of the reasons why I got involved in the development side of things years ago. I was working in Glasgow in the late 1970s and went with some colleagues to look at an Alexander 'Greek' Thomson block on Eglinton Street. In those days although

"The combination of new courtrooms for the city with commercial units and flats is certainly unusual but Parliament Square is just the sort of urban weaving that requires the Buredi light touch. For the residents its an address to die for."
Ian Wall

"Much of what The Burrell Company has done is innovative, often combining conservation with clever new-build to create something fresh, modern but linked inextricably with the fabric of the city. There are few developers who understand cities better".
**Malcolm Fraser,
Malcolm Fraser Architects**

Parliament Square, Edinburgh

Mackintosh's name had become synonimous with Glasgow. Greek Thomson was still relatively unknown.

The Eglinton Street building was a fabulous, complete tenemental street block. When we looked around it, it was in good condition, apart from some subsidence affecting one of the stairs on the rear elevation. This, apparently, was the excuse for knocking the whole thing down. I was horrified and felt that the building should be saved and brought back into use. However I was warned off, told quite firmly by my superiors that it was a Council matter and would be dealt with by them. Looking back it's quite clear that they wanted to widen Eglinton Street. The irony is that, after more than twenty-five years, the site is still derelict. They knocked down one of Greek Thomson's last major domestic works and didn't even have the decency to tarmac over the site. I still feel guilty for having backed down under pressure.

My warning off was effective because at the time I was an employee of a government agency. I didn't have the nerve to say, "Stuff you!". Perhaps some of the conversion and restoration work we've done since then is a little bit of recompense for letting that one go. I could have done something. Being involved in the Gorbals was going to be another bit of payback, but the net result, after ten years, is yet another derelict site. It is, after all, much easier to commission a masterplan every two or three years than to actually do something constructive on the ground.

THE EDINBURGH END OF THINGS was really starting to work for us. Buredi, having started in Dublin Street, had proven its worth. We could work as a team, there was real excitement in the process and the product was pretty good. We came out of that project thinking we should do more. We were acquiring Coalhill so we pitched for a few other projects which had come onto the open market. Parliament Square was being sold by the Council and we bid for it against quite a number of other developers. It was a funny sort of development package because it wasn't simply a matter of buying a site, the old police station and converting it. It also involved taking on the District Court buildings adjacent to the police station, refurbishing them and leasing them to the Council.

Parliament Square worked. The Festival Fringe was interested in the basement and ultimately moved in and we introduced a restaurant and shops to the ground floor. It's a nice mix of uses, very appropriate to it's setting on Edinburgh's most historic street. There are some lovely large apartments and, because we were working around retained features on one side of the development, we followed that design cue with panelled doors and mouldings. On the other side of the close, an area which had been used for storage, there were no remnants of the historic architecture, so we gave it a contemporary feel.

Parliament Square was the latest part of the whole Tron Square regeneration. We had started, back in the 1980s, with Old Assembly Close. Over a decade later we were engaged on the second phase at Parliament Square. A few years on we would be handling the final bits of what was to become known as the Tron and which was, all in all, a fairly complex bit of urban weaving.

Another complex project, this time a single building, was the former Dental Hospital in Chambers Street. The consortium that was looking at the former Edinburgh Royal Infirmary buildings was struggling with the Dental Hospital. Morrisons, the main player in the consortium, asked us if we would consider undertaking a joint venture..

There were some pretty horrible pieces of equipment in the lower floors of the building. It was the usual mess of boilers and so forth, but we were jammed between a bank and the Sheriff Court and were very aware of our neighbours. We didn't want to disturb or annoy them if possible.

The final layout was ingeniously planned by Lee Boyd. The ground floor entrance effectively divided into three. The right-hand door went through to the rear giving access to the restaurant and down into the basement for the bar and kitchens. The door on the left went to a reception area and upstairs to first floor offices which we sold to the Royal

Chambers Street, Edinburgh

26

"The challenge was to create enough flats to make the thing stack up from a development point of view and to find a technical solution which allowed it to be built within a sensible cost. We struggled over the concrete versus steel frame issue. I reckon we were devilishly cunning to get more flats out of the site than anyone else."
Richard Murphy

"Buredi's second outing with a Richard Murphy designed scheme was utterly compromised through the planning process. With the best of intentions they insisted that the scale of what was proposed for Belford Road be drastically reduced and that it should give the appearance of being stone-built, quite at odds with its design and structure. So now we have a truncated building clad in obviously ersatz stone. The real frustration was the loss of the over-sailing glass roof. Had we retained the height, the cost could have been justified. Instead it has a teflon sail which, though unusual, is a compromise. So the residents and perhaps more importantly, the city, are the losers."
Ian Wall

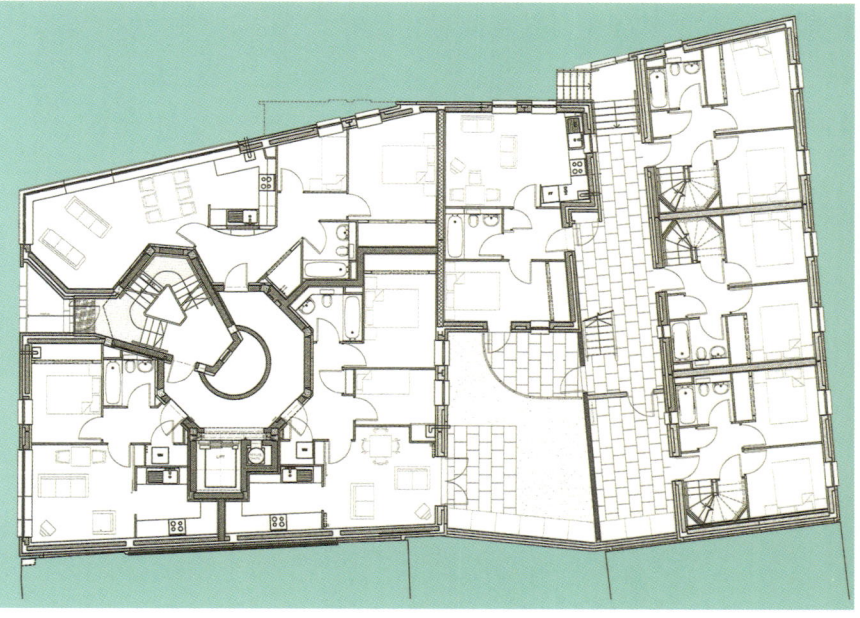

Belford Road, Edinburgh

Museum who had built their new museum across the road but didn't have enough administration space. The central door opened on to the existing circular stair which went up to the residential apartments on the second floor and above.

Some of the best spaces from that development were on the upper floors. Being a dental hospital the building had a lot of natural light. People were very keen on moving in. As it was a listed building we were allowed to build without associated car parking. There had simply never been any car parking attached to the hospital. Some critics reckoned that the lack of parking made the development unmarketable. In fact the apartments went pretty quickly.

We had acquired the Dental Hospital with Morrisons and again joined with them in a consortium to put together proposals for the whole of the former Edinburgh Royal Infirmary site. Allan Murray produced the masterplan and the development team was EDI, Morrisons and ourselves. The bidding process was long and tortuous and then, at the eleventh hour, we were told to ignore the previously stringent conditions and asked how much we would pay without any conditions attached. One of our consortium couldn't meet these new requirements and it would appear that the decision was made largely on that premise and we missed out. As it stands the purchasers brought in Foster & Partners, arguably the UK's best known architects. The scheme, which is now under construction, is undoubtedly very strong.

THE NEXT SCHEME UNDER the Buredi banner was at Belford Road. Our architect, Richard Murphy, produced a very intriguing design which increased the number of units which the site would otherwise have accommodated.

The way in which Richard's design was structured, which probably wouldn't be allowed now, just a few years on, created an open stairwell with natural ventilation. Richard's internal plan was, as ever, extremely clever and helped to make the site stack up commercially. At the end of the piece we got a very good building, but not as good as it might have been.

Belford Road would have been an even better building had we not had to endure a sort of imposed planning blight. The original proposal had a glazed tower. This was an extremely elegant solution for a prominent corner site. As everyone knows corners require real skill and what Richard produced was a solution with just the right urban scale. However, the planning officials decided that we had to chop a storey off it then, in response to complaints from the neighbours, they asked us to take off another storey and, of course, when it went to the planning committee they didn't know the second storey had already been chopped off so they asked us to remove yet another storey.

The truncated design which was ultimately built still looks a lot better than everything around it but nothing like as elegant or sophisticated as we had originally intended. The compromises demanded inevitably gave us something less appropriate and much more like a standard block of apartments. Its pretty ironic that the buildings which flank our block, which got their planning permission ten years previously are mediocre in the extreme. At one stage, the scheme was hugely over cost and we almost abandoned the whole idea. The situation was saved by house price rises which made it a bankable proposition. It's a very nice building, but not as good as the one we wanted to build.

A FURTHER RICHARD MURPHY SCHEME for a problematic Edinburgh site is the Tron, probably one of the best crafted developments we've ever done. Effectively the housing component is part of a collection of sites, all within Edinburgh's World Heritage Site, and all innovative. On reflection, as I have already observed, the Tron development started with Old Assembly Close and included Parliament Square and the Court building. What became the Tron housing development was actually a Council owned, double height, car park which they refused to do anything with for

Tron Square, Edinburgh

Greyfriars Hostel, Edinburgh

many years, largely because it was the car park nearest to the City Chambers and used by councillors and senior staff.

The situation changed with Councillor David Begg's election. This was prior to his involvement in central governments' congestion charging and other traffic policies. The local authority owned more car parking spaces in the centre of town than anybody else and the irony was not lost on the press. The situation led to some embarrassment and a determination backed by Councillor Begg, that the Council should get rid of part of its car parking pool.

We decided that the Tron development should be a competition. We've never been keen on huge competitions where hundreds of architects put in an enormous amount of work and there's only one job. Instead we ran a restricted competition which seemed to make a lot more sense. The judging panel, chaired by Professor Isi Metzstein, included Piers Gough and Janet Street-Porter.

Understandably the process was fairly lively. At the end of the piece the panel was torn between Richard Murphy's scheme and Allan Murray's. The two proposals were very different but both very good. The final conclusion was a sensible compromise. It was felt that Richard Murphy's scheme which, as ever, demonstrated his genius for internal planning, had the edge. However, we knew that the replacement for the Cowgate Nursery was the next component of the overall Tron scheme, so we were able to award that job to Allan Murray.

What's really important about the Tron is the extraordinary land assembly task which preceded the competition itself. The fact that the children's nursery, then in the Cowgate, was in a most inappropriate position, with a playground literally a couple of metres away from a busy road, with all the dangers and pollution that implies, prompted the process. A new site for the nursery was identified, behind our High Street office in an open space where the Old Town dustmen used to park their barrows. In recent years it had been used extensively during the Festival, but for the other forty-nine weeks of the year was only really visited by winos.

Prior to clearing the site and building Allan Murray's superbly designed nursery, we encountered a bit of a problem. The former Wireworks building, which had been part of our Old Assembly Close acquisition, had been sold on by ourselves some years before to the Faculty of Advocates. They objected to the nursery on environmental grounds. Their objection was that the noise of human beings, particularly toddlers, would disrupt their august deliberations. Clearly they had overlooked the fact that they were right in the heart of a city and, therefore, you might expect some noise from the neighbours. Maybe they didn't realise that the toddlers would be indoors most of the time and, anyway, weren't really such a bad thing. We won. The Faculty backed down. The kids have their nursery.

The demolition of the Cowgate nursery freed up that site for another Richard Murphy building which is being undertaken by Castle Rock Housing Association and EDI. This will provide the affordable housing component.

The whole Tron Square process has been an extraordinarily protracted endeavour, but well worth it. Over a period of twenty years we have renovated some buildings, demolished others, created new-build elements and shifted the various parts of one of the most densely used areas of Edinburgh around to produce a whole series of fairly consistent buildings which mesh together. The overall result is an exercise in land assembly and provides a considerable return for Edinburgh.

The Tron endeavour is a great example of working with an individual, the late David Cownie, in the local authority who actually maintained his interest throughout. In the end the city has gained affordable housing, a new nursery, got rid of an ugly car park and achieved some superb pieces of new design. Richard Murphy's Tron building itself has to be the highlight. Working on the historic rig system of the Old Town Richard created what is effectively two buildings with a glazed link connecting them. As elsewhere, we designated the basement and ground floors for offices and restaurant

use with residential above. Predictably the flats at the top get superb views.

NOT SO FAR AWAY FROM the Tron, again in Edinburgh's Old Town, is the former Traverse Theatre and Greyfriars hostel. Greyfriars was being worked on by EDI as part of the process of improving accommodation for homeless people, getting away from the Dickensian, cell-like spaces that they had lived in for decades.

As EDI was going ahead with Greyfriars and we were proceeding with the Traverse, which we bought on the open market, we brought the two projects together under the Buredi umbrella to make one larger, more sensible scheme. We got planning permission for a small hotel at the Traverse, a beautiful group of buildings, very similar to Tailors' Hall, entered through a pend giving onto a little enclosed courtyard. However the Council became uneasy about the notion of licensing the space. The fact that we were proposing to convert a Listed building and open it to the public didn't seem to be a factor. Ultimately they just wouldn't budge.

So we couldn't create what would have been a little gem of an hotel in the very building where, according to many accounts, the Edinburgh Fringe was born. The only option left was residential. The flats, more or less, sold off-plan, confirming our experience that people are really keen to live in the city centre. It's another piece of the regeneration of the Grassmarket which, over the past thirty years, has gradually risen from being fairly tawdry and neglected to a lively characterful place, maximising the benefit of its historic buildings (with the exception of the lost opportunity of the Traverse Hotel!).

HAVING DISCOVERED OUR ENTHUSIASM for joint ventures with Buredi, our next major step was to form a joint venture company with the Murray Group. That came about because we had been building up a whole series of projects. It takes a very long time to move almost any regeneration project

CITY ✚

URBAN SPACE

Drumsheugh Gardens, Edinburgh

Schaw House, Bearsden, Glasgow

Elmhill, Aberdeen

City Hospital, Aberdeen

forward. So its perhaps inevitable that every so often, when things start coming together, you realise that you have an unmanageably large portfolio which all requires funding at the same time.

Putting all our projected schemes together with those of our other joint ventures we realised that financing and handling the whole lot at one time might be just too much for us. We had been talking to David Murray's Premier Property Group (PPG), about a joint venture in Glasgow. Their feeling was that a one-off project was not really of interest but that they were excited about a deal on a larger portfolio. So we brought eight projects to the table and the deal was done.

Our joint venture with PPG seems to work pretty well. With 'Premier Burrell' we are working on Ravelrig in Balerno, City Hospital and Elmhill Hospital in Aberdeen, two phases of Mitchell Street in Glasgow and Mount Zion at Quarriers Village, also in the west. Late additions to the mix were two former nursing homes, one in Drumsheugh Gardens in Edinburgh and Schaw House in Bearsden. Once up and running we added a further project to the portfolio, a hotel in Gullane, East Lothian and have several other projects under consideration.

Drumsheugh and Schaw were our first direct acquisitions for Premier Burrell Limited. Both sites were negotiated from the same vendor. Both had been nursing homes but fell foul of changes in legislation with regard to fire escape provision and access.

Drumsheugh was ripe for conversion, very much akin to what we had done with Castle Terrace many years before - converting buildings back to residential apartments. Drumsheugh is good quality property in the West End of Edinburgh, although over the years it had lost some of its features, including one of its internal staircases. Schaw, on the other hand, is a true conversion as the building was originally designed as a hospital. The variety of spaces is intriguing. It is a spectacular Tudor Gothic design, appropriately grand for Bearsden, looking south over the Glasgow skyline with amazing spaces which create remarkable apartments.

Premier Burrell is not set up as a joint project, rather as a joint company. Its name gave us a fairly distinguished sounding development company without resorting to the cut and paste approach of Buredi. Something else worth mentioning about Buredi is that the name came about not only because 'Edibur' sounded pretty crap but because Ian Wall, who always sees the marketing opportunity, spotted the word 'red' in the middle of the name. This would, he thought, give us a great graphic design opportunity. Of course, we insisted on taking control of the graphics. The logo is blue and green!

Part of the Premier Burrell portfolio is in new geographic territory for us, but otherwise a fairly familiar style of development, at the City and Elmhill Hospitals in Aberdeen. Over the last few years, with their functions being supplanted by newer buildings, both of these historic structures gradually became redundant, until they were being used for little more than storage.

As these two buildings sit within large swathes of fairly attractive landscape we were fearful that both sites would be snapped up by the volume house builders and we would be excluded. Partly through the sheer scale of their operations and partly because they tend to build fairly standard house types, these guys can build a lot cheaper than us. To overcome the problem we linked up with the Stewart Milne Group, which is well established in Aberdeen, to bid jointly on these sites and a few others.

Elmhill is an elegant classical building. One of its claims to fame is that it was reputedly hit by a bomb in World War II. The fact that hardly any bombs landed on Aberdeen and that Elmhill sits in the middle of landscaped gardens made this a quite remarkable misfortune Sadly it destroyed most of one wing of the classical main façade.

In converting the building into residential use, we proposed rebuilding the bomb damaged bit. We initially promoted a contemporary approach which could have looked stunning and would, in a sense, have acknowledged the history of the building. However, the planners took

exception to that idea and insisted that we build a replica of the original. They don't quarry granite in Aberdeen anymore so we had to import it from China to rebuild the bomb damage and make it look like the original. Sadly Aberdonian and Chinese granite do not look similar, even to an untrained eye.

As agreed Stewart Milne created the new housing around Elmhill. The same is the case at the City Hospital. There, we converted a group of buildings all, again, to residential. At City we demonstrated our remarkable marketing creativity. Stewart Milne, reflecting the regenerative effect of their endeavours in the area, called their part of the project 'Renaissance', with each block carrying the name of a great Renaissance artist.

Faced with the conundrum of how one might promote wards three and four and the administration block of the former City Hospital, we applied our finely honed marketing skills and came up with the names "City Hospital" for the overall development and 'Ward 3', 'Ward 4' and 'Admin Block' for the other bits. We rather liked the concept and we carried it into the graphics with a big red cross of photographs on a white background.

CARRYING ON THE DESTRUCTIVE THEME from the Elmhill bomb is another recent endeavour at Ravelrig House in Balerno. Until this one we had a proud record of never losing a building to fire, flood or natural disaster. However, we lost this one. It was while discussions were in progress, but before we actually took it on, that somebody decided to burn out the building. It was a former children's home and maybe someone had a grievance about their upbringing and decided to exorcise their feelings with a touch of pyromania.

At the end of the piece we got a burnt-out shell. We managed to hang on to most of the walls and rebuild with new wall-heads, a new roof and a completely new interior. It's more or less what we would have done anyway but at a lot more cost. We also converted the stables and other

Ravelrig, Edinburgh

Vienna Apartments, Mitchell Street, Glasgow

outbuildings, but overall it gave us a fairly modest eleven units. The architect was Glasgow-based Gareth Hoskins, who brought some great ideas and produced something that is just right for the setting.

One further and intriguing part of the Premier Burrell portfolio is Vienna Apartments in Mitchell Street, Glasgow. Glasgow City Council promoted an initiative to look at the upper storeys in buildings which were underused, unused or even derelict. We looked at a block running between Union Street and Mitchell Street excluding the ground floor shops and managed to secure the upper floors for conversion into office suites and apartments.

On Mitchell Street itself there was a big brick box formally occupied by a health club. The building had no architectural merit so we knocked it down to clear the site. The idea is to put a new building there by Gordon Murray and Alan Dunlop Architects which, alongside the converted upper floors of its near neighbour, will help to bring a significant scale of residential property into an area that, until now, hasn't seen much of the growing trend towards city centre living.

The site is adjacent to the Lighthouse, 'Scotland's Centre for Architecture, Design and the City', in central Glasgow. Although the Merchant City and some other areas have been regenerated, this one is lagging a bit behind. We have high hopes for its future.

AN EXTREME CONTRAST WITH Mitchell Street is Quarriers Village near Kilmacolm. This superb Victorian planned settlement was built to house orphans from Glasgow. Now that the onus of care provision is on local authorities, charities like Quarriers have moved into other activities. Their perspective is that their role is to care for people and not buildings. Quarriers had already sold on the former school building for conversion. The next, inevitably more contentious, property was Mount Zion Church. The building, which can hold two thousand, had a congregation of about twenty folk before its closure.

Churches are always very difficult to convert, not least because in many instances the contents of the sanctuary are of real merit. At Mount Zion the importance is more about the external form of the building and how it fits within the structure of the village. Given that we proposed a solution which would respect and preserve the externals of the church, we got the agreement of the planning officials and Historic Scotland.

However, churches are also emotional icons. Quite a number of people who were not in the regular congregation decided that they really needed a church. They didn't use it – and they certainly weren't prepared to cover its cost – but they really needed it. The congregation themselves had been offered alternative premises but, understandably, they also wanted to hold on to their church. The practical issue was that Quarriers were spending many thousands of pounds every year maintaining a vastly underused structure.

Because the campaign was well orchestrated, the planning committee decided to refuse the application. This certainly wasn't the sort of problem that they regularly have to grapple with. The meeting where Mount Zion was discussed had an agenda which consisted of a couple of satellite dishes, a bungalow and the church. Out of all of those, the only potential vote loser was the church.

Councillors have a tendency to shy away from making decisions where there's a risk of losing votes so planning decisions tend to become more problematic in election years. That happened to us at Elmhill where, when the decision to convert went to appeal, the reporter found one hundred percent in our favour. At Quarriers, even without a local election looming, the committee wasn't minded to approve.

The BBC ran a series of programmes on what to do with redundant churches, and used Mount Zion at Quarriers as an example of what happens when some people still want to worship there. It's an emotion versus economic conflict. On balance it was a reasonably fair programme. At the planning appeal, the Reporter supported our application

so the development is progressing. We've also added other acquisitions in the village to our portfolio though not another church, I'm glad to say.

ON THE SUBJECT OF CONTENTIOUS projects, one where we really came in for a drubbing in the press, was Caledon House in Edinburgh. This job had a particular poignancy for me as the building was where I worked in my first job in Edinburgh after qualifying as an architect. I wasn't there for very long and it was a perfectly pleasant place to work. The building was, therefore, quite undeserving of the retribution which I meted out after we had acquired it. We immediately knocked it down to build a fairly modest and, I think, elegant, block of flats.

At the time of our barrage from the press on this one, I was in Syria visiting my son who was studying there. This was in the pre-mobile phone era (certainly for Syria) so nobody could get in touch with me. I travelled to Lebanon for a few days and on the outskirts of Beirut, I phoned the office. I have to say that Beirut was a fairly surreal setting to be informed that we had made the front page of the newspapers. The site was going to be shut down because one of the neighbours maintained that we had moved the building several metres from where it should have been built.

The allegations, if true, would have resulted in the building sitting in the middle of the road. In fact we had moved the building a fairly nominal distance to protect some trees and further away from the neighbour, not nearer as they contended. They had also argued that the building was taller than the planning permission allowed, whereas we had actually reduced its height. But the press had a story and, although it was based on completely inaccurate junior geometry, neither the neighbour nor the Council would back down. This farce ended up in a great furore.

Learning all this from shell-torn Beirut had a certain piquancy. Here I was, in a city where people were struggling to rebuild their shattered lives, and back home we were

Caledon House, Edinburgh

Madelvic, Edinburgh

embroiled in a front page, headline news, struggle based on absurdity.

At the end of the piece the Caledon House issue went to a series of council committees. Nobody wanted to admit that the whole thing was based on a miscalculation which had been taken up by the press. It had become something of a political football. The fact that we were suffering financially didn't seem to be a factor. At the end of the piece, to save face, the Council granted a supplementary planning permission which approved the re-siting of the building so peace and harmony were restored. Caledon House was duly completed and I'm sure its residents are very good neighbours.

I'M NOT SURE IF Bangour Village in West Lothian is contentious – probably simply problematic. Sadly it has yet to get off the ground. This project started many years ago with the housebuilder Beazer. It has taken so long that, in the interim, they became some other company which then became Persimmon. Effectively however, the idea was to have a volume housebuilder looking at the new build and us at the existing buildings. It was being marketed by the local health trust who had built a new hospital, making the historic village buildings redundant. We set about trying to put together a masterplan that would be acceptable to all parties. For reasons that fail me this process has gone on for many years and, in the meantime, the buildings are falling into disrepair.

I reckon there may be more listed buildings on this site, than in the rest of West Lothian put together. You would imagine that the local politicians would want to give this site real priority. As a developer, you can only put in your best efforts. When your proposals are rebuffed again and again, you begin to despair. Inevitably your focus is diverted elsewhere and you move on to other projects.

A MORE RECENT EDINBURGH SCHEME, much less contentious than Caledon House but with fascinating origins, is Madelvic. This historic group of buildings in Granton was marketed as part of the Edinburgh Waterfront regeneration. We heard on the grapevine that it was being promoted with the intention of attracting developers with a proven track record in sensitively dealing with listed buildings. Despite twenty plus years of doing just this in Edinburgh we hadn't been approached. However, we eventually secured the project.

The Madelvic Factory is renowned as Scotland's oldest car factory. In fact it didn't last very long as a car factory, only two or three years, and its two, solidly built, rectangular blocks subsequently went through a whole succession of uses, including serving as a torpedo factory during World War II. The vendors wanted the building converted for commercial use but, in our view, the area is not ripe for that at present.

We came up with the concept of live-work units which have been successful elsewhere. The idea is to utilise the ground floor, which doesn't have a particularly good aspect to the outside but will open onto an attractive internal courtyard, as offices. From the ground floor, via the courtyard, residents can access the upper floors which will provide the residential space. It's a nice idea but we haven't the least clue whether the market will take to it.

The architect for Madelvic is Malcolm Fraser, whose Edinburgh-based practice has produced some pretty stunning, award winning, work. The street-edge of the development will be finished with a contemporary commercial block which will serve as both a protective wall and a buffer to the converted historic buildings behind. We have brought in a specialist provider of sheltered housing for rent so hopefully we'll have a mix of ages and various uses, which should help to kick-start the fairly ambitious plans for the regeneration of this whole area.

Upper Strand, appreciably larger than Madelvic, and all new-build, is probably our most significant recent project. It was won as the first release in a design/developer competition that was run by Waterfront Edinburgh, a company fifty percent owned by the Council and fifty percent by the local enterprise company. They have assembled the land, created the masterplan and committed to building the infrastructure.

The competition process for this site required us to interpret the original Llewelyn-Davies overall masterplan and the more recent Page and Park area masterplan. For that we brought in Elder & Cannon, Reiach and Hall and Ushida Findlay. Prior to our submission we had been approached by the Places for People Group who were keen on expanding into Scotland and wanted someone with local knowledge to join with. We admired their approach to housebuilding, which gives credence to design, mix, tenure and accessibility – not the typical housebuilders' approach. Consequently we formed Upper Strand Developments and commenced on site in late 2005.

Because of the size of Upper Strand, in excess of 500 dwellings, we gave ourselves a challenging brief, but one that couldn't easily be tackled on a much smaller scale. The development incoporates designs by various architects, builds upon the detailed masterplan and urban design exercises, employs contemporary detailing and materials, achieves high energy standards, utilises a district heating scheme, underground parking, bus and tram stops, city car-club spaces, underground rubbish collection and recycling areas, home zones and CCTV.

There is good chemistry between Places for People and ourselves which was picked up both by the architects and by the vendor in awarding us the scheme. We certainly hope this development will set a marker for the regeneration of the area as a whole. There are various other projects coming along in the same area including further phases by Wimpey and Barretts and a number of other larger housebuilders.

ANOTHER FAIRLY LARGE CURRENT undertaking is in Manchester. When we had our first foray into England in the late 1980s, we could see that what we were building in Scotland had a great deal of potential for a number of key cities south of the border. However, when the recession hit, we retrenched to our own patch to lick our wounds.

Assembly Street, Edinburgh

"It is remarkable that after 25 years they are not only still going, but are still restless – interested and interesting".
Malcolm Fraser, Malcolm Fraser Architects

"Most developers are all promises at the beginning then things start to go awry. Happily, The Burrell Company is one of the few exceptions to this unfortunate rule".
Piers Gough, CZWG

"Burrell is still leading the charge. It's a pity that the revolution they helped start in the residential field – has been slow to move into the architecture of commerce".
Gordon Murray, GM+AD

In retrospect, we should have been looking harder south of the border, where a large number of initiatives were at play and a great deal of public money was being used to promote urban regeneration. Ironically, many of our schemes were being quoted as exemplars. Unfortunately nobody actually asked us to take part in any of the resulting projects so, through the 1990s, we did nothing in England apart from the odd skirmish to keep the morale going.

We now have a scheme in Ancoats, Manchester called Murray's Mills. This one seems rather appropriate. It was a couple of Scots on the make in the late eighteenth century who went to Manchester and built what were some of the first truly industrial settlements on the banks of the soon to be opened Rochdale Canal.

The mill buildings must have been incredible at the time. They were seven or eight storeys tall. They were the first buildings to be gaslit and had the latest, steam-powered, engines. This was cutting edge technology and very much at the forefront of the industrial revolution.

Now that they are past their sell-by date as mills, the local building preservation trust was given financial support to restore the shells and stabilise the buildings. Again our involvement in this project started as a design/developer competition, this time in partnership with another company, appropriately called Inpartnership. So Duncan Sutherland (Chief Executive of Inpartnership) and myself are the present day Scots on the make. Together with a Mancunian architect who made his name in Scotland, Richard Murphy, we plan to restore and convert them into a variety of uses. There is a residential bias but we also plan a significant amount of office space, live/work units and an hotel.

Hopefully Murray's will be the forerunner of many developments south of the border. We have bid for other projects and, as always, it takes some time to adjust to local market conditions but, alongside Inpartnership and others, we're always on the look-out.

BACK ON OUR HOME TURF there are various other projects in the offing. Our five current joint venture companies are embarking on new projects, whilst The Burrell Company has enlarged its direct development side and continues to bid jointly with developers throughout Scotland.

Premier Burrell has acquired a derelict listed building, formerly an hotel, in East Lothian to convert to residential use. Upper Strand is progressing, whilst Places for People and Burrell are looking at a number of opportunities, particularly in the west of Scotland. Most recently Burrell have teamed up with John Sheridan's Classical House to form Classical Burrell and have a number of projects under option.

The Burrell Company's own direct developments include an initiative in Edinburgh as a response to the fact that house prices have increased so much in the last few years. A lot of people who are trying to get on to the housing market are struggling. We set about creating some units within a listed former metalworks and adjacent site that would be very suitable for first time buyers in Leith. Our architects, Sutherland Hussey, have come up with some ingenious plans. Unfortunately, despite being used by Architecture and Design Scotland as an exemplar, it took us four attempts to get planning permission with the outcome seemingly dependant more on which way the wind was blowing rather than planning policy.

Hawkhead, Paisley, has also taken years of planning but is, hopefully, approaching realisation. This is another project in which Burrell is responsible for the existing Listed buildings (with Elder and Cannon as architects) whilst a house-builder, this time Keir, will look after the new build. A former infectious diseases hospital might not seem the most promising start. However, the separate pavilions on this site are superb examples of the work of Thomas Tait from the 1930s, the period of that distinguished architect's greatest achievements.

Fountainbridge, part of the Scottish and Newcastle Brewery complex on the northern edge of the canal, southwest of the city centre, is at the heart of Edinburgh's newest financial district. Allan Murray has produced a superb design which, strangely enough, fits perfectly into the masterplan for the area. Mind you, given that the council commissioned Allan to do the masterplan, that might not be so odd. It will link two well-established residential areas with new connections, including a new street (Freer Street) and a new bridge over the canal, through a formerly closed-off industrial landscape. It will also transform the canal into much more of a leisure asset. This is a substantial work of urban design and could help revitalise a large swathe of the city.

On a much more modest scale, Bell's Mills on the Water of Leith, near the Dean Village, has superb potential for housing. It took a long while to negotiate because the access to the site is pretty awkward. Finally, the scheme went into the planning committee with a recommendation for approval. It would certainly have produced excellent housing. Unfortunately, despite complying with all the local plan guidelines and policies, this was another case where local residents orchestrated a well organised, anti-campaign and where the Councillors, as ever concerned about their vote, rejected the proposal.

We had to take it to appeal where the logic of our proposal and the benefits of saving an historic building were endorsed. We also got a considerable award of costs. So, all in all, this cost the public purse a load of cash and us a year of delay. It does seem odd that when we have fairly clear planning legislation and even if you work within the priorities, a vociferous minority, whose interests are very clearly 'not in my back yard', can create all sorts of damage and even condemn important historic buildings to dereliction or demise.

A happier scenario altogether is Coalhill II, once again an inspired Buredi name for the extension to our original Coalhill I development. Its acquisition from the Council was tied in with a new rough sleepers' initiative as a mechanism for releasing funding to provide better living conditions in a separate development in an adjacent building. It's all new-

Bell's Mills, Edinburgh

build again, and as with the original Coalhill is designed by Allan Murray, with affordable housing encircling a communal courtyard and with the basement floor given over mainly to car parking.

LOOKING BACK AFTER MORE than twenty-five years in this game, there are some surprises, some failures and some successes. Most surprising to me is the dearth of architect-developers – although we were at the forefront of the movement in the early 1980s it's been a lonely existence. What has definitely happened, however, is that whilst we were one of a handful of developers who would encourage and promote young designers, more developers are doing so every year. Perhaps there is no need for architects to become developers nowadays in order to achieve their design ambitions.

The failures have been outweighed by the successes I'm glad to say, leading to the greatest success: we're still in business.

Looking forwards (always the exciting bit!), the nucleus of our team – John Forbes, Raymond Ross, Lindsay Russell, Natalie Rintoul and myself have nearly 100 years of experience of working together between us. Our joint ventures are with a great bunch of people. Our order book has never been so full. The competition has never been greater – but that's part of the buzz.

There are a lot of challenges to face in the coming years, most notably in how to integrate our urban regeneration experience with the goal of zero carbon housing, the short-term likely demise of much of our existing housing stock and the perennial issue of affordability.

After twenty-five years it doesn't get any easier. Mind you, the very nature of our business has been about taking on the awkward sites. We have spent quarter of a century on projects which might help mend the weave of Scotland's city centres. There is a concensus that the standard of housing development in Scotland has improved greatly in recent years. We like to imagine we have helped in that process.

We have acquired historic properties that no other developer would have looked near and tried to combine practicality with a respect for what their original architects were telling us from across the years. We have worked with talented young architects – many of whom are still with us a quarter of a century on, though no longer quite so young. We still try to nurture new architectural talent.

We have also tried to be innovative, to encourage good architects to create great architecture, to promote a masterplanned approach wherever appropriate and to give people better and more stimulating places to live in.

We remain confident that the challenges ahead can best be met by employing excellence in design within the wider context of sustainable development. Our success is evident from the number of developers who have adopted our approach – more competition for us, but good for Scotland.

We are well aware that our game is about keeping up the energy levels, sheer dogged hard work and a good deal of luck. So fingers crossed…

Fountainbridge, Edinburgh

Coalhill II, Leith, Edinburgh

Carrick Quay, Glasgow

THE BURRELL COMPANY ACQUIRED the Carrick Quay site, overlooking the River Clyde, as part of a company buyout. The name reflected the fact that the MV Carrick was, at that time, berthed alongside. There were schematic designs by the architect Dai Rees whom Burrell invited to participate in a limited competition with four other architectural practices invited to make submissions. Forbes and Burrell judged the Davis Duncan scheme to be the most appropriate. Quantity surveying advice was for a more 'strong if forward' design solution, but this was, thankfully, ignored. Having said that, the scheme was somewhat ahead of its time for Glasgow City planners, who did their utmost to change and dilute its impact.

The implementation of Carrick Quay was in tandem with Balfour Beatty. Appropriately, given the proximity of the river, the scheme incorporated nautical references including crows-nest like balconies and mast-like elements. The loss of a Scottish Development Agency grant seriously affected the financing of the project which was also hit by the recession of the early 1990s. However, the block has subsequently been completed with a new hotel which follows the design cues of the original. The development still makes a bold statement on Clyde Street.

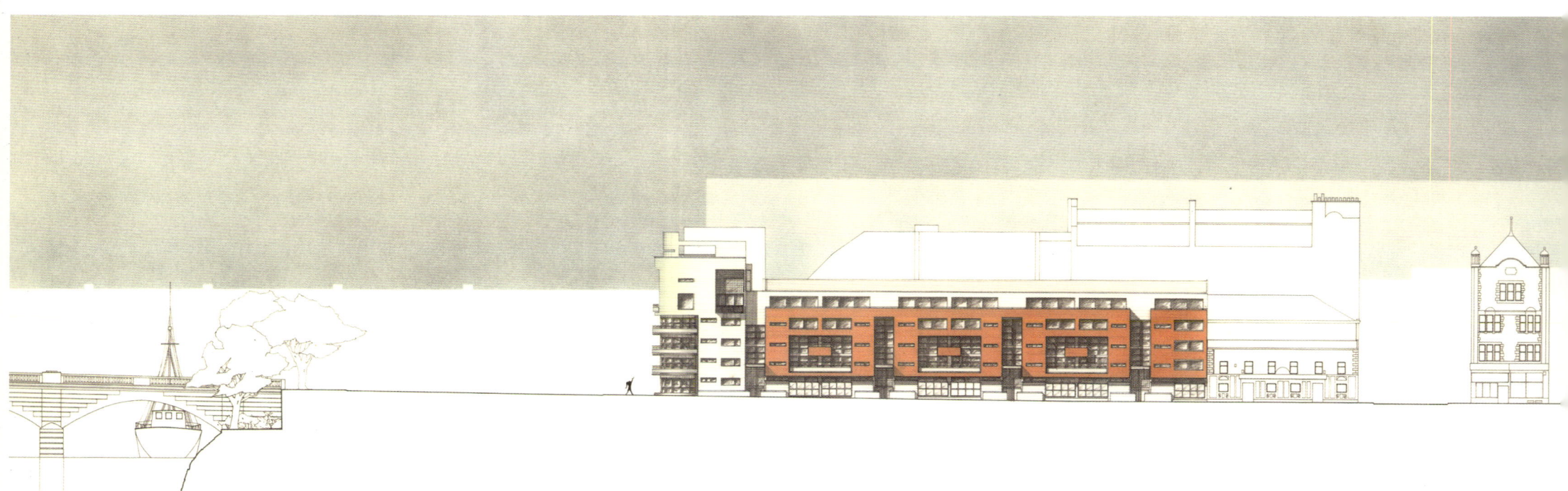

THE ARCHITECTS' JOURNAL

27 FEBRUARY 1991/£1.25

NEWS/Prison guidelines out
Nightmare on liability street
FEATURE/Poland's new dilemma
BUILDINGS/Designing for fossils
PRACTICE/Setting up in Spain

Ingram Square, Glasgow

THE REDEVELOPMENT OF FOURTEEN existing buildings within the heart of Glasgow's Merchant City was one of the most significant events in the regeneration of the whole of central Glasgow. Initiated by Kantel the development was undertaken by a joint venture company established with Glasgow District Council and the Scottish Development Agency. The initial drawings were by Kantel and included some elaborate treatments for the new-build elements by Andy Bow. However architectural consistency was introduced by the retention of Elder & Cannon to work up the whole scheme and deliver the successive phases. In total the development delivered 240 flats, student accommodation, offices, 20 shops, parking for 108 cars and a large communal garden.

The building which set the whole thing in motion was formally known as the Houndsditch, a 'B' Listed, early Victorian, academic exercise dating from 1854, designed by John Baird and R W Billings. The latter's considerable fame as an architectural historian, with a particular interest in traditional Scottish buildings, is evident in the highly unusual treatment of the building's original facades.

The Houndsditch presented particular challenges. Ultimately it was reworked as a façade retention with three storeys set behind the retained frontages onto Brunswick and Ingram Streets. The scale rises to four storeys facing onto the courtyard and garden behind. This internal space also gives onto a substantial subterranean car park.

As it evolved the significance of Ingram Square towards re-establishing a vibrant residential community within central Glasgow was increasingly recognised. The various warehouse buildings which had been rescued from dereliction sit alongside infill sections which, while displaying the resolutely post-modern attributes of the mid 1980s, are carefully judged in scale and form against their neighbours and achieve the notable trick of re-introducing brick to a major Glasgow city central scheme without jarring.

Ingram Square's significance for Glasgow and indeed in the wider UK context was acknowledged in two major cover features in the Architects' Journal and in numerous awards. It also prompted a whole series of listed building residential refurbishments. It does not seem too much to boast that this project was the first major step in regenerating what has now become a major leisure and tourism focus for Glasgow – and one of its most popular residential areas – The Merchant City.

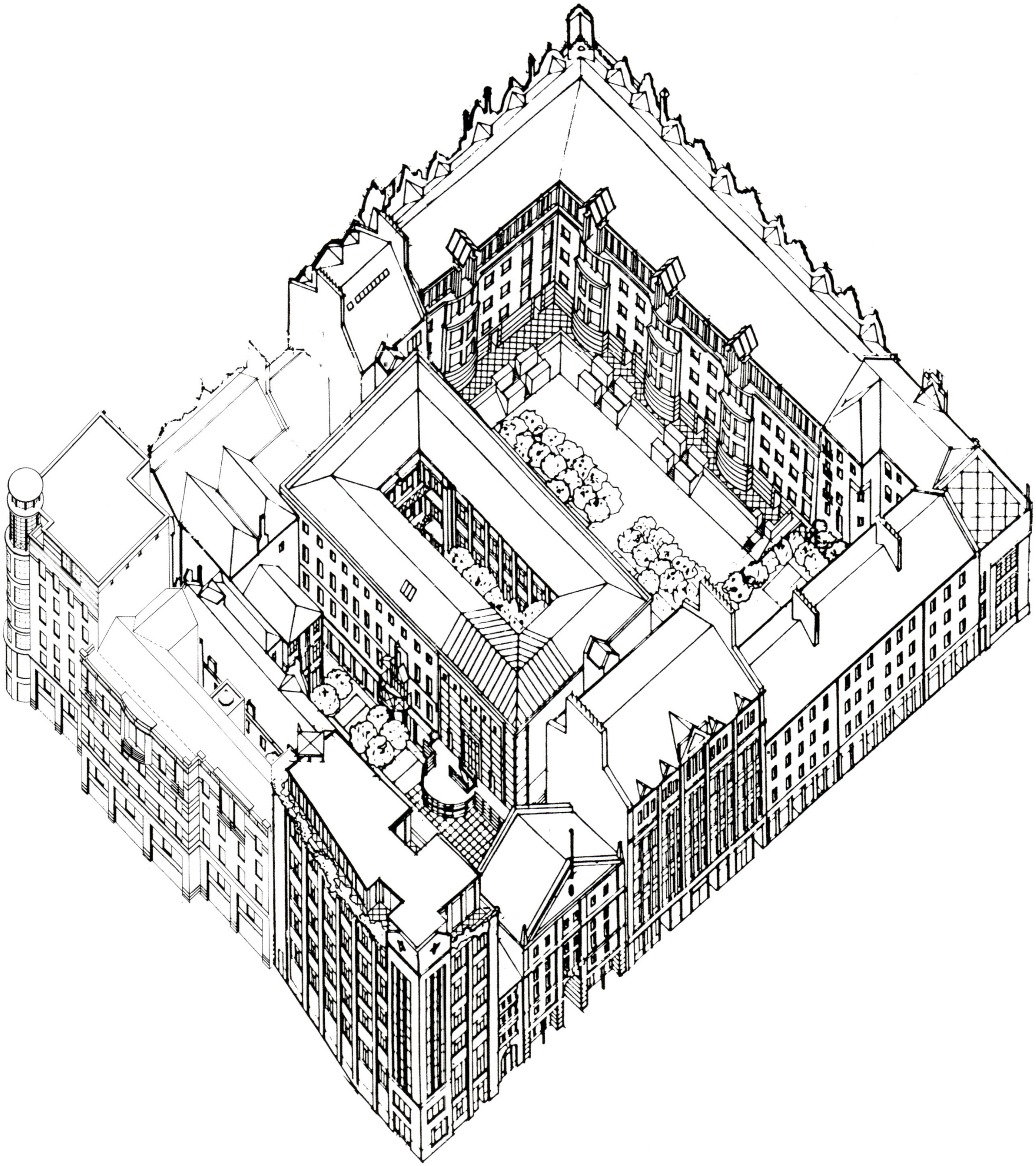

WILSON STREET
INGRAM STREET

WILSON STREET
INGRAM STREET

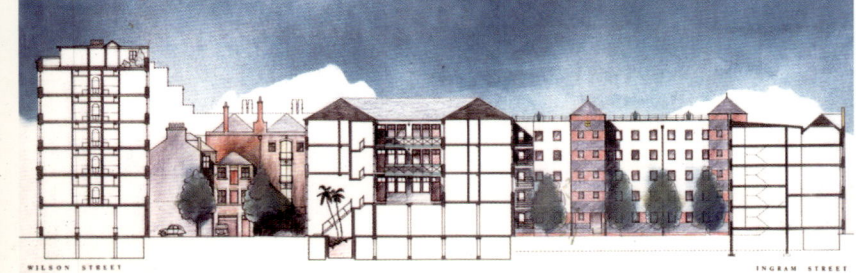

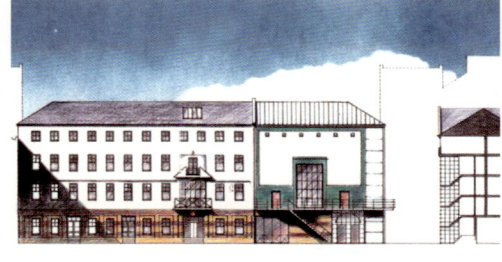

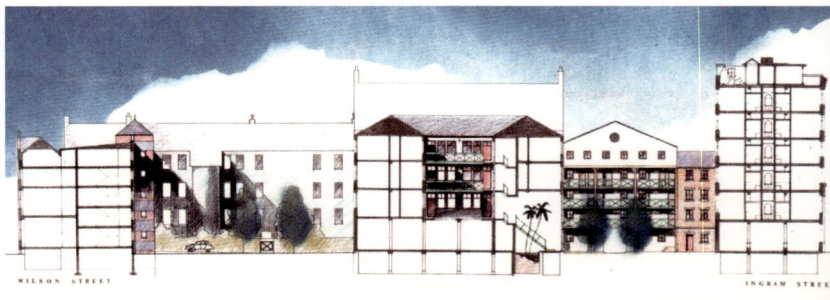

INGRAM SQUARE

"We were determined to avoid pastiche but equally we knew that overt modernism would never convince the planners. This was, after all, a very unusual combination of refurbishment and new-build and a huge investment in the area. We decided that, while we could get away with being playful with the facades, we should be pretty restrained with the roofscapes. To avoid splitting the existing tall windows with the horizontal banding of new floor levels there were lots of mezzanines. This was low cost housing which really kick-started the regeneration of the Merchant City."
Dick Cannon

"On a project of the scale of Ingram Square, with the extraordinary problems it threw up, I suppose a claim from one of the contractors was inevitable. It was the first we had ever received and thoroughly intimidating. I remember John Forbes phoning me to ask what it looked like. He has reminded me many times since of my response – "it's A4 in plan... and about two foot high!". Happily, despite this amazing volume of paper, the whole thing got settled without too much acrimony."
Dick Cannon

Glasgow Tower Competition

THE IDEA OF PROMOTING a new viewing tower for Glasgow was generated in discussion with Stuart Gulliver, then Chief Executive of the Glasgow Development Agency. The intention was to create a high-profile design opportunity for Glasgow and a new icon for the city with comparisons being drawn with other iconic viewing towers, particularly M. Eiffel's Parisian masterpiece.

We sought out an appropriate city centre site, initially proposing the junction of the High Street and Ingram Street – potentially a bold termination of this long vista. However, the GDA's preference was for St. Enoch Square. The Glasgow-based landscape practice Gillespies and Building Design magazine were persuaded to become co-sponsors and Neil Baxter Associates were invited to promote and co-ordinate the international competition.

Launched in July 1992, the competition sought "to generate ideas for a tower – a landmark – in recognition of Glasgow's dynamic past, in celebration of its rejuvenation, and most significantly, as a symbol of the city's confidence and aspirations for the coming century". In total, it attracted 353 entries from all over Europe. The judges, Stuart Gulliver, Lord (then Sir) Norman Foster, the internationally renowned engineer Anthony Hunt and David Mackay, another renowned architect from Barcelona, along with the then Director of Planning for the City, Jimmy Rae, eventually settled on Richard Horden Associates' proposal which "works well at the domestic level of the Square" as well as providing a "sculptural contribution to the city's skyline".

In time, Horden's design, whose materials and scale related to those of the St. Enoch Centre, would be transferred to an exposed site adjoining the Glasgow Science Centre, a Millennium project to which it added a third element in addition to the Centre itself and its IMAX cinema. Unfortunately, the extraordinary technical innovation of the Horden design, this was to be a tower which revolved on its axis, created real problems, perhaps exacerbated by the exposure of this new site. It was built, and stands as a proud sculptural object but sadly has never really worked and, for most of its life to date, has been closed to visitors.

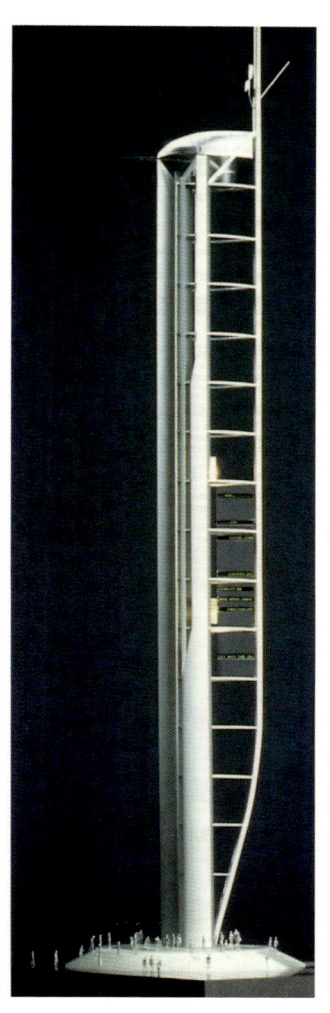

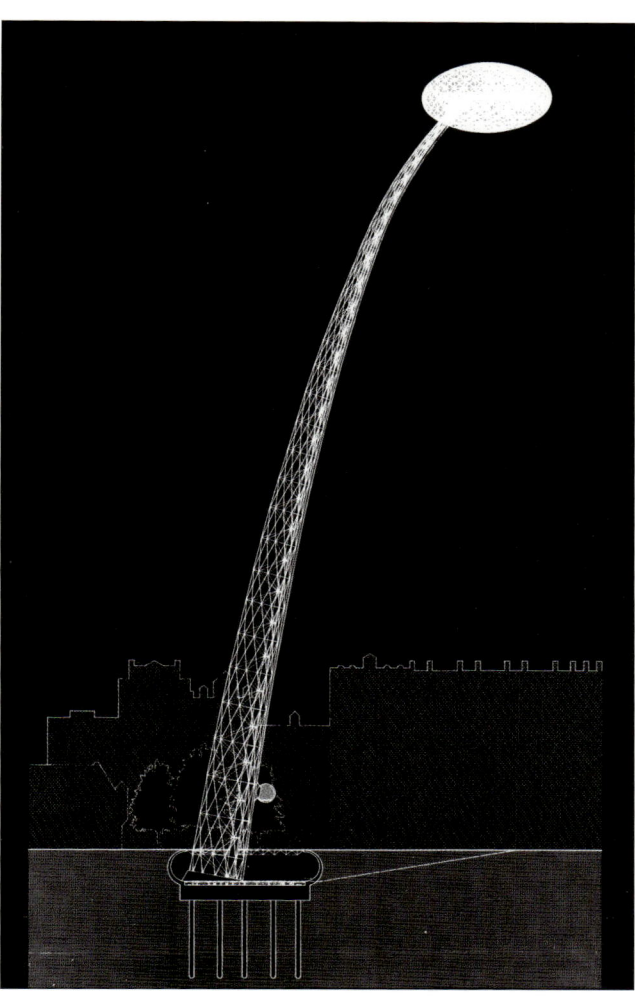

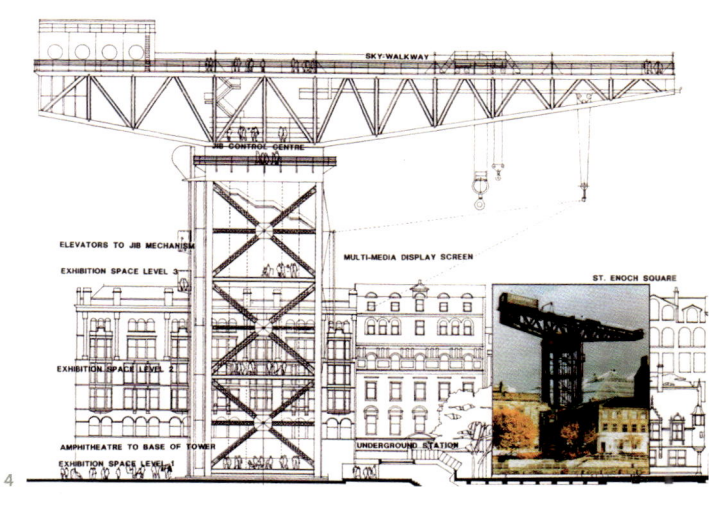

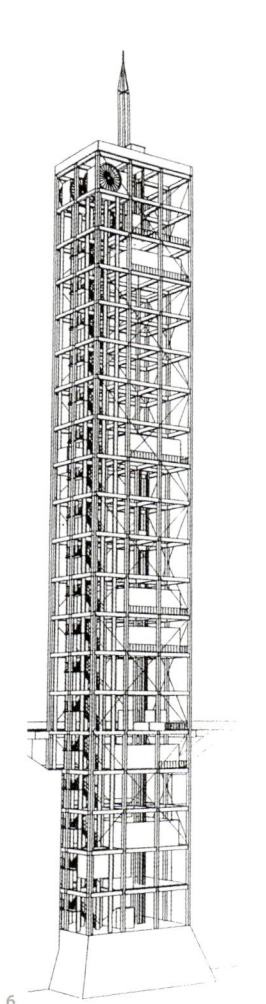

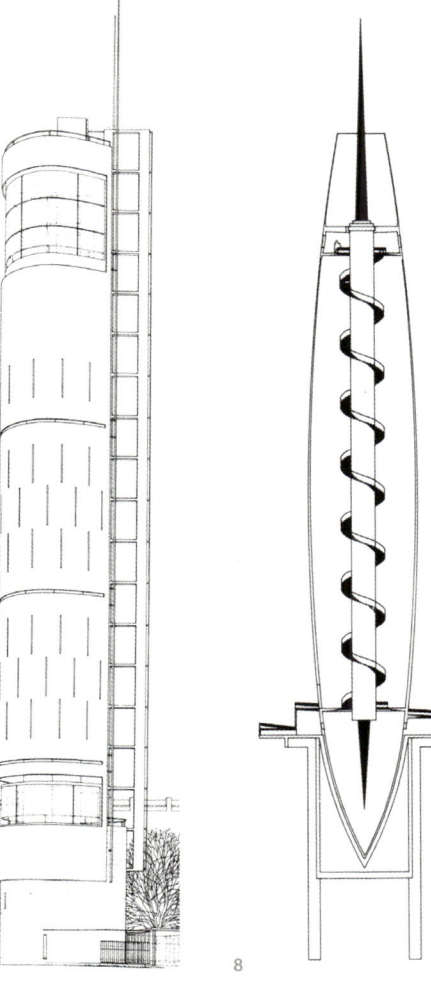

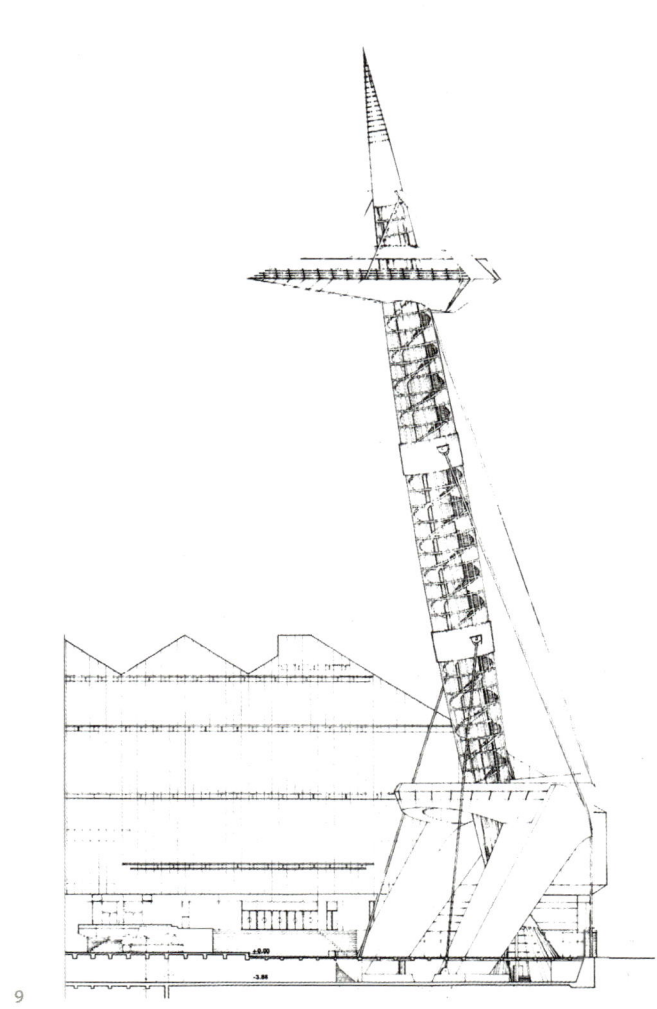

Dublin Colonies, Edinburgh

AT THE TIME OF THE Dublin Street Development Duncan Sutherland was still Chief Executive and Ian Wall had recently joined EDI. The notion of EDI and Burrell working together had arisen after a number of meetings between Ian and John Forbes but the Dublin Street project was the first occasion when the introduction of Burrell Company expertise to an EDI project was sought.

The site was in Dublin Street Lane. Bill Ross of EDI had run a limited architectural competition which had been won by Richard Murphy. The scheme, in keeping with the scale of the area, proposed relatively modest low-rise, two storey, housing with the occasional three storey section. EDI was having real difficulty making the thing stack up financially. The Burrell Company was invited to engineer a solution.

On the whole the changes were relatively minor. Expensive underground car parking was deleted and further traditional apartment homes introduced to the scheme. Some of the internal apartment layouts were also refined in the process. However, one major change was the demolition of the neighbouring, redundant, brick warehouse which provided a site for six, two storey, townhouses. This introduced not only a greater variety of accommodation but greatly improved the appearance of the development and its contribution to the townscape.

With these refinements the scheme went on site. Although there were problems with aspects of the contract and the project overran by a year on what was supposed to be a one year programme the development was hugely popular and received major credits, including an RIBA Award.

As a test case to see if EDI and Burrell could work together Dublin Street worked extremely well. Murphy's plan, his first major residential scheme, reflected the design of buildings from the original Broughton Village giving a very organic appearance to the overall development and the impression that this was something which had evolved within the existing fabric of the area. In this respect we delivered a 'twist' on the distinctively Edinburgh 'Colonies' type development – homes entered at ground and upper levels with external staircases.

While the planning was organic the use of white render, cladding with over-sailing roofing, galvanised staircases and balconies was radically different from what had been there before. The balconies punctuated otherwise fairly simple building forms. In the groundscape a cobbled surface provided a simple, traditional solution appropriate to a mews-style development and the perfect foil to the contemporary materials of the buildings themselves.

Homes for the Future, Glasgow

THE MOST SUBSTANTIAL DEVELOPMENT under Glasgow's City of Architecture & Design 1999 banner was the residential exhibition project which carried the inspiring epithet 'Homes for the Future'. The 1999 Director Deyan Sudjic wanted to create a "state of the art" housing development which would help regenerate an area of need. After some time a site was selected in the east end of the city, overlooking Glasgow Green.

The competition process was unusual with developers asked to choose their architects from three separate lists, local, national and international. The Burrell Company selected McKeown Alexander from Glasgow, Richard Murphy from the national list and Ushida Findlay from the international list. The McKeown Alexander and Ushida Findlay schemes were successful and subsequently became major components of the Homes for the Future development.

Ushida Findlay's design was an unusual, narrow, stepped block overlooking the Green with commercial space in its ground floor. McKeown Alexander produced a terrace and a building to sit on the rearmost point of the site, as a sort of exclamation mark. The Burrell Company added its own marketing spin by naming these the 'Flagship' and the 'Object' buildings respectively.

Other contributors to the overall development included Rick Mather from London and Elder & Cannon and RMJM from closer to home.

The Homes for the Future development was extremely successful from the point of view of the publicity it created and the rapidity of sales it generated. However, the necessity for a rapid programme resulted in major problems. The time available to construct the development in preparation for the planned exhibition of a number of selected apartments led to Burrell engaging a Management Contract. This turned out to be highly unsuccessful, hugely problematic and very, very costly.

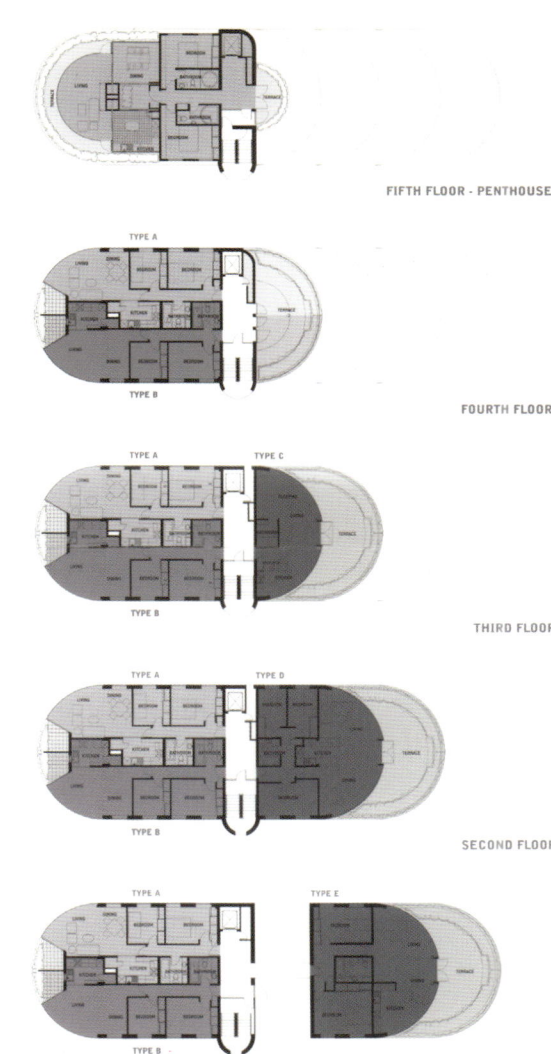

FIFTH FLOOR - PENTHOUSE

FOURTH FLOOR

THIRD FLOOR

SECOND FLOOR

HOMES FOR THE FUTURE

"We were incredibly optimistic and, in retrospect, incredibly naïve. It was a nightmare, the timescale was far too tight, the procurement very problematic and, to cap it all, we had to liaise with a Tokyo based architect for our flagship building. The whole thing was a disaster from a developer's point of view but a huge success for Glasgow which won loads of awards. "
John Forbes

"I suppose my credentials as an 'international architect' for Deyan Sudjic's list were questionable. Forfar's international status is debatable! Fortunately however, I was practicing in Tokyo at the time and married to a Japanese architect, so I think that got us over the line."
Kath Findlay

"The Burrell submission was by far the best in terms of responding to the client's requirements to involve local, national and international architects yet achieve something which had integrity. Despite that integrity, however, we got bumped – such is life. But it would have been much better if they'd built our scheme too."
Richard Murphy

"At Homes for the Future Burrell gave us our first real opportunity on an international stage. We were trying a lot of new ideas and it was the synergy between Burrell and ourselves that really made it happen."
Henry McKeown

Coalhill, Leith

EDINBURGH WAS BIDDING FOR the City of Architecture Award for 1999. Ian Wall was working with the City Council's Estate Department and receptive to a proposal from The Burrell Company. John Forbes suggested that The Burrell Company should organise an architectural competition to ensure a higher quality of architecture, appropriate to Coalhill's prominence within Leith and contributing to Edinburgh's 1999 bid. The site was also reputed to be that of one of Scotland's first parliaments. Another house builder was negotiating with the City for the site but the competition idea won the day.

The competition, for an ambitious mixed-use development, was organised to challenge three Scottish practices based in Scotland against three international Scots. Among the international grouping were Ushida Findlay from Tokyo and David Mackay in Barcelona (the latter's Scottish credentials were admittedly questionable but the fact that he had lived in Scotland for a period was deemed sufficient qualification). The competition was judged by a distinguished group, including Piers Gough.

The competition process was anonymous but such was the apparent 'signature' style of the winning design that, without even opening the envelopes, John Forbes phoned Elder & Cannon and congratulated them on their win. Unfortuunately when the envelopes were opened it was revealed that Allan Murray's design style was not a huge remove from what Elder & Cannon might have drawn and

Murray was in fact the winner. The ensuing phone call to Elder & Cannon, asking them to re-cork the champagne, must qualify as the most embarrassing of Forbes' life.

After delays resulting from poor cost advice the project was put into a fundable shape. While the corner oval block was originally designed as offices the decline in that market resulted in a change to residential. The road was closed to create a wharf-side environment beside the Water of Leith. The scale of the buildings was such that it was agreed that pedestrians should be able to move under them, which created the planning difficulty of ensuring that the area was permeable without creating dark spaces or concealment. Another regeneration initiative was the proposed conversion of the adjacent Leith House as accommodation for 'rough sleepers'. This project was undertaken jointly with Dunedin Housing Association in tandem with various environmental improvements and the second Coalhill development, the imaginatively entitled Coalhilll II.

The first phase of Coalhill created a number of small, single aspect studios within the oval block. Despite some unease about how these might sell they went very quickly. It is also ironic that the necessity of converting space originally designed as offices for residential use led to very dynamic residential plans. The building featured in various magazines and won the accolade of Best Apartment Block in the UK for 2001 from National House Builder Magazine.

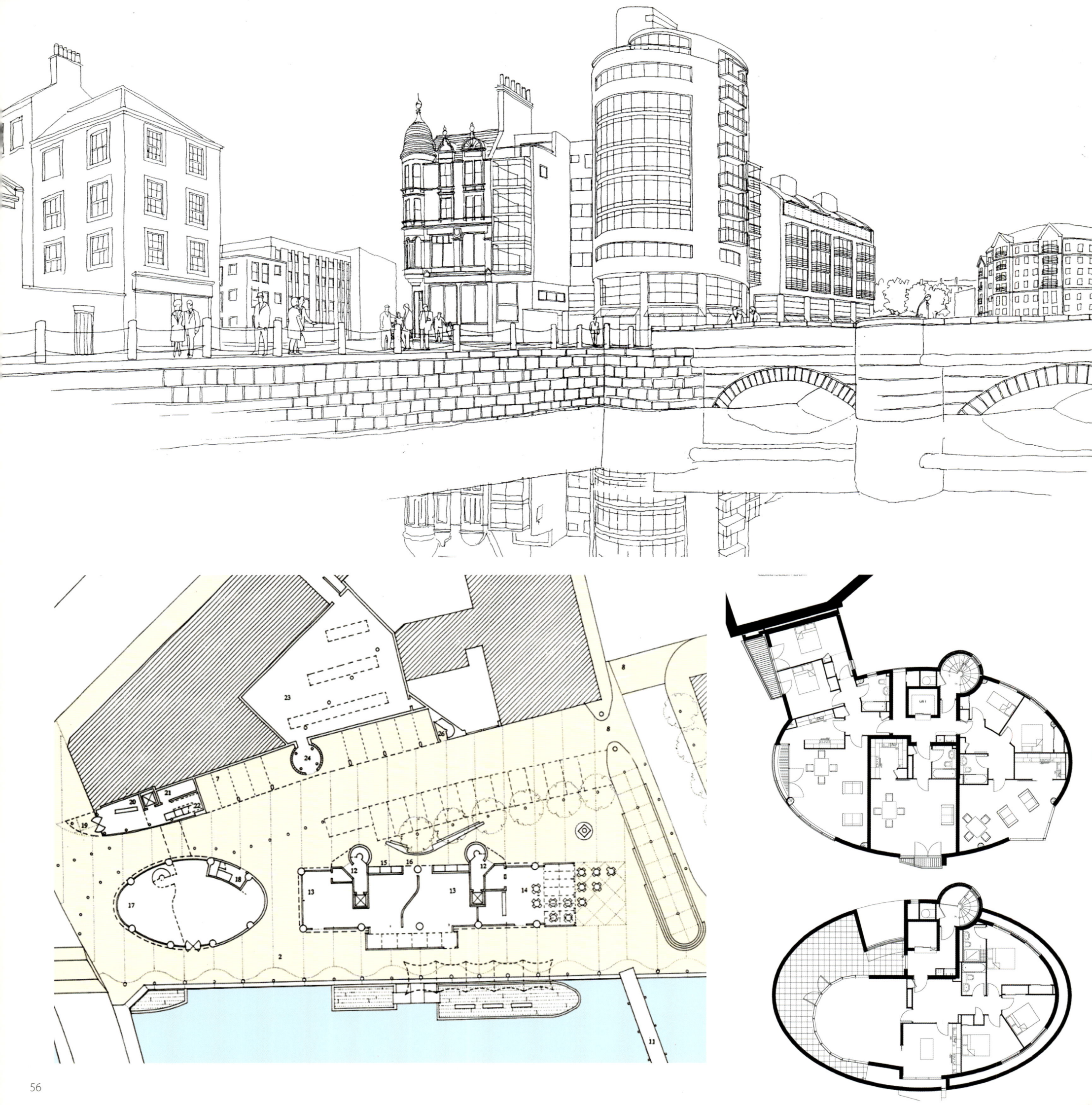

"All I asked at the outset was that Forbes and Burrell should put me on their list of competitors. At Coalhill the competition was stiff, including Elder & Cannon from the west, Allies & Morrison from London and Mobel Bohiegas Mackay from Barcelona. Our approach was 'crash and burn' – we had nothing to lose, hardly any work on the books and felt that challenging the brief was the only honest response. Our idea was to produce something which, rather than blending in, would be boldly differentiated from the buildings around. It would also require closing the street. We wanted to pull up the quality of the area by creating a powerful statement. Fortuitiously, our very sound architectural reasoning for producing two buildings also made good development sense by allowing the phased release of new apartments onto the market. We won and then the fun began…"
Allan Murray

"One thing I have always appreciated about The Burrell Company is their enthusiasm for architectural competitions. Coalhill was a demanding brief for a site that really needed something special. It produced something quite different from what Leith had seen previously. This was a real Buredi triumph and what's been built in the area since testifies to its success."
Ian Wall

Tron Square, Edinburgh

THE TRON REGENERATION PROJECT came together as a result of a complex series of acquisitions. Firstly Burrell approached the City to acquire the former car park site on Old Fishmarket Close. This had been owned by the City and used by councillors and officers. Adjacent to the car park was the semi-derelict, People's Palace, formerly a rough sleepers hostel, which had recently been acquired by Castle Rock Housing Association. Discussions were ongoing with Castle Rock on various projects, notably the re-location of the Cowgate Nursery from one of the most polluted streets in the city to a more appropriate location.

At the same time Burrell was looking at opportunities around Tron Square, including a series of derelict sheds behind the company's head office on the Royal Mile. EDI had been talking to the company about the potential reuse of a small car park on the Cowgate, After extensive and complex legal negotiations with the Council it was agreed that the nursery would be relocated to the site of the derelict sheds behind Burrell's offices, that the cleared nursery site would provide new offices and housing on the Cowgate to maintain the urban scale of this important route, that the Old Fishmarket Close car park would be demolished for new housing and that the People's Palace would be restored.

This was a very complex property deal. It was remarkable that it all came together to very positive effect. Of course the benefits to the city included highly visible urban improvements, new terraces and squares and the improvement of the City of Edinburgh's own housing stock within the original Tron Square.

These ideas came together in a very loose design brief which was promoted as a limited competition. The judges were chaired by Professor Isi Metzstein and included Piers Gough and Janet Street-Porter as well as representatives from the Council. The judging process was protracted and difficult and despite Izi Metzstein's power of personality it took a great deal of discussion to reach a conclusion. At the end of the day Richard Murphy won the housing element and Allan Murray, whose scheme for the same site was not dissimilar, was awarded the nursery. The headmistress of the nursery, initially resistant to the bold plan of the building, came round and ultimately was completely thrilled with the new nursery.

Richard Murphy's new housing was simple in plan form with two narrow building blocks, one set forward of the other, on either side of the recreated close. The buildings are tall and narrow with two apartments per floor in each block, linked by a narrow glazed connection over the close. Interestingly Murphy's design was the only one with a pitched roof submission and, intriguingly, he told us after the event that he had only decided to enter at the last minute, giving his office only a day to draw up the ideas. The idea was sound and, fortuitously, they had a brilliant draughtsman who was happy to engage in that architectural classic – an all-nighter – to produce the competition winning scheme. Not only did the design win the architectural competition it was later to pick up many awards.

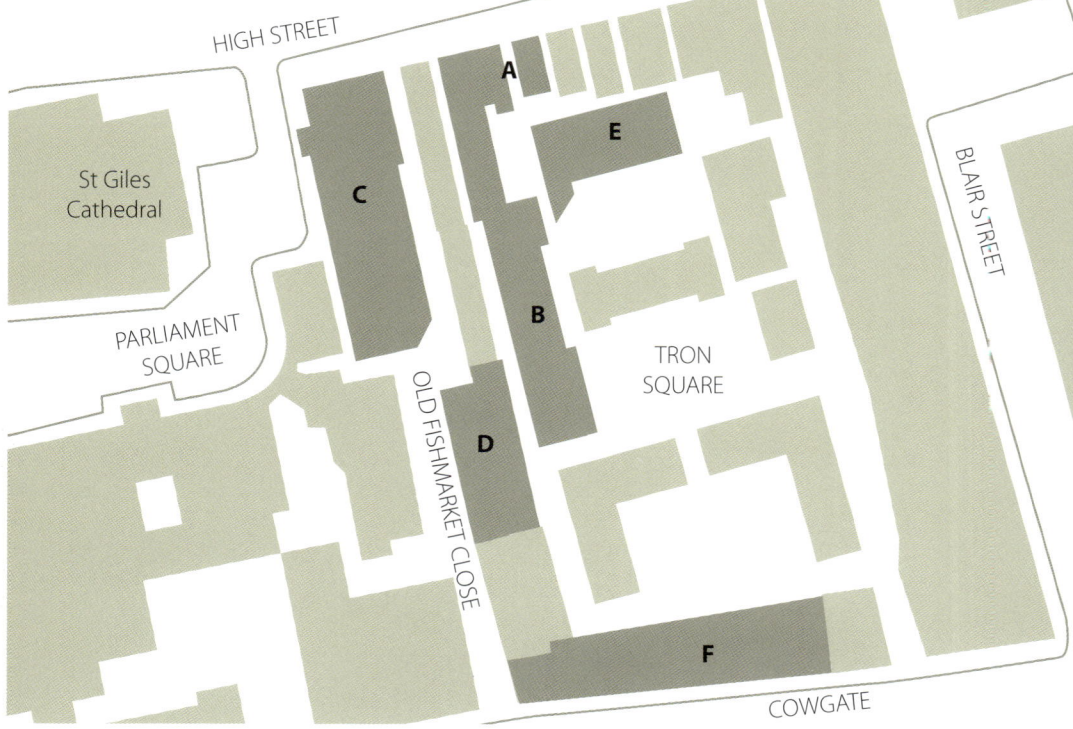

A Mixed uses, Old Assembly Close, Simpson & Brown

B Faculty of Advocates, Benjamin Tindall Architects

C No. 1 Parliament Square, Jenkins & Marr

D Housing, Richard Murphy Architects

E Nursery, Allan Murray Architects

F Housing for Castle Rock Housing Association, Richard Murphy Architects

"The brilliant land-swap deal meant that the Council lost a carpark and gained a nursery. Burrell organised a limited competition and happily our approach, which recognised the history of the area, won."
Richard Murphy

"Another competition winning design, Tron Square, is an extraordinarily intelligent reworking of the Old Town's architectural history. It was also the culmination of a protracted and complex process of site acquisition, reprovisioning and careful urban surgery. It's tough enough dealing with one site but when you are working on three at once, each dependant upon the other and each having its own unique timing and cost constraints even getting things to add up is a nightmare. Achieving award winning architecture was a bonus, in part attributable to the design competition and undoubtedly Buredi's special achievement – the proverbial icing on the cake!"
Ian Wall

Ravelrig House, Edinburgh

THIS SITE WAS THE SUBJECT of an open market bid. Burrell submitted a joint offer with Bryant Homes proposing that we would undertake the conversion of the existing buildings, and Bryant the new development within the grounds. Although this joint offer was successful the issues of new-build close to an historic house and in a highly sensitive area were much deliberated by the planners. It took several years before consents were granted.

The existing buildings were of limited architectural value so the proposal was to add interest through their conversion rather than simply produce a faithful restoration. The newly established, Glasgow-based, Gareth Hoskins Architects were engaged. At the time we commissioned them there were only four people employed in Gareth's office.

The day before the purchase of the site from Barnardos was finalised, disaster struck. The main house was burned out. The event was notable: the only building we have ever lost to fire in twenty-five years as developers. Unfortunately it precipitated a protracted re-design and negotiation through the loss adjusters.

At the end of the lengthy process of converting the Ravelrig buildings the houses are impressive. Substantially glazed new extensions enlarge the spaces while the existing buildings open up to create bright contemporary interiors. The larger houses incorporate double height volumes and mezzanines. The building also features numerous roof lights which create highly attractive, top-lit, rooms. There is a certain irony that the Ravelrig process took so long that by the time it was completed our architects were far from a fledgling practice. In the interim they had accumulated numerous accolades and awards and had risen from their relatively modest beginnings to a staff of thirty-six.

Upper Strand, Edinburgh

THIS MAJOR PROJECT, WITHIN a planned 20,000 person settlement, addresses the first phase of Edinburgh's waterfront. The Council established Waterfront Edinburgh Limited (WEL) to promote this crucially important regeneration. A masterplan was produced by Lewellyn Davis Architects and Page & Park. This, in turn, led to an architect/developer competition. One of WEL's wisest early moves was to select the joint submission by Burrell and Places For People as the winning scheme. This will deliver 500 homes, alongside leisure, retail and offices, over the next five years.

A new square, Saltire Square, will sit alongside the boulevard being created by Elder & Cannon and Reiach and Hall. This responds to the parkland setting into which the development is being placed. Relatively informal in its architectural treatment and rising to a fairly modest four storeys, it forms a new street, with the elevation which addresses Caroline Park House being designed as a contemporary classical terrace. Reiach & Hall is also creating an eleven storey tower which will incorporate a bar/restaurant at ground floor level. This will serve as one of a number of "exclamation marks" within the overall masterplan. The balance of the Reiach & Hall contribution is set within a more formal streetscape and is, therefore, designed to reflect this more urban location.

This development will establish a new standard for sustainable housing in Scotland. It incorporates a district heating scheme, recycling facilities, underground car parking provision and rubbish collection. Just as Glasgow's Ingram Square was a model for urban regeneration in the 1980s, this major Edinburgh development is the way forward for urban expansion.

B. Allen 02

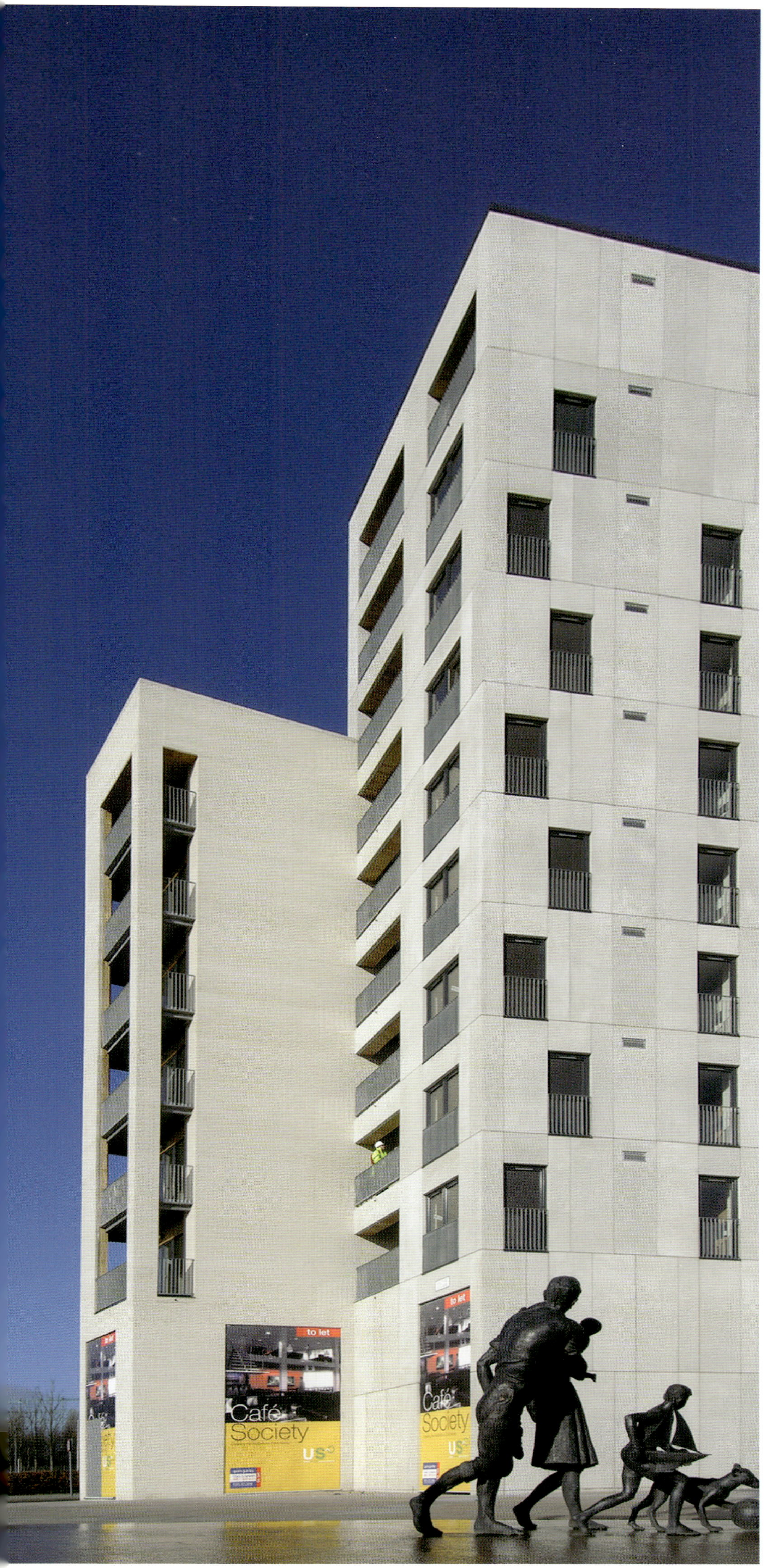
to let
Café Society
to let
Café Society

VISIT US
WWW.UPPERSTRAND.COM
APARTMENTS FOR SALE

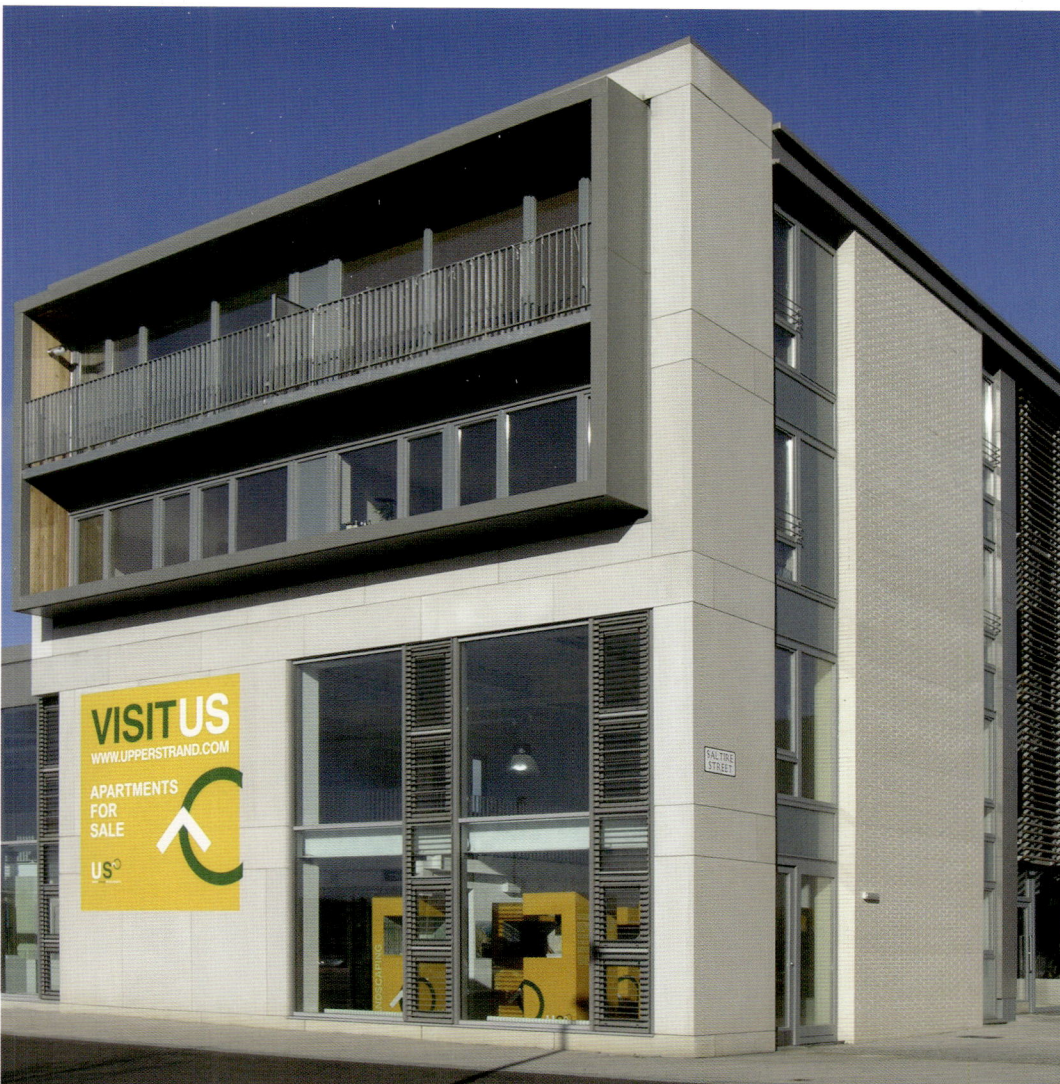

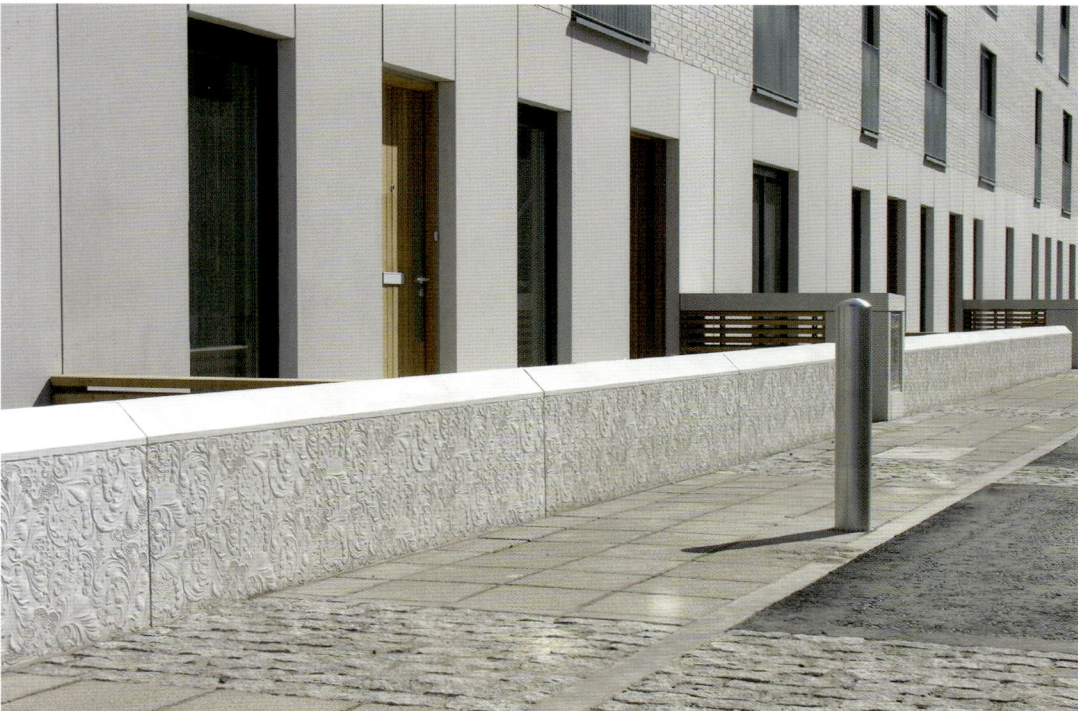

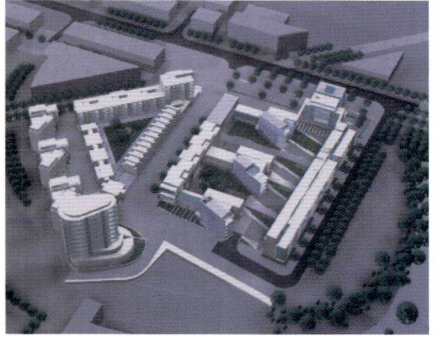

Drumsheugh Gardens, Edinburgh

THIS SERIES OF LISTED former townhouses at 21-23 Drumsheugh Gardens in Edinburgh's West End presented a relatively straightforward exercise involving the removal of various additions and internal conversion to provide, generally , two bedroom apartments.

Working with Smith, Scott, Mullen Architects the broad approach was to retain as many of the internal features as possible. Where new interventions were introduced, these were undertaken in a contemporary manner. This work included new kitchens with screen walls, often located as a free standing object set within the larger, historic, volume. The initial idea had been to treat these pieces almost as furniture, cladding the outer skin in a suede veneer. This unusual appraoch was abandoned as it was thought that potential purchasers would not appreciate it.

Amongst a considerable variety of plan types for such a relatively small development, perhaps most notable was the smallest house in the scheme. Originally reserved as a bin store in the first plan, the area evolved into a main door, studio house, with a sleeping loft, and a total area of 38sq. metres. This added bonus sold at a handsome figure!

These buildings had evolved with operating theatres as part of an earlier hospital use. Curiously, these had required large glazed windows to the north façade. As these were located at the top floor level the views were spectacular. This was fortuitous for the two newly created apartments. One in particular also features a massive roof light that floods the living space with light.

However, by far the most impressive spaces were found at first floor level in what were termed the 'Drawing Room Apartments'. Here, the high ceilings, generous windows with floor level cills, ornate plaster work and new hardwood floors created memorable spaces.

Schaw Hospital, Bearsden

AT THE FORMER SCHAW HOSPITAL in Bearsden, just outside Glasgow, the challenge was particulalry demanding. An unusual symmetrical plan, with ancillary buildings to the rear, the building had been much altered to serve as a nursing home. The external façade is remarkable, with a tall central tower that is a landmark in the townscape. The building sits within extensive landscaped garden grounds.

The proposals to convert the building to apartments were fairly straightforward on paper. However, in practical terms there were significant difficulties. The basement level did not enjoy good light. New lightwells were created and plans were continually modified to make the best of the evolving environment. The grand entrance hallway and broad corridor dictated the plan arrangement.

As this was an important listed building Historic Scotland was anxious to ensure that as much of the original fabric as possible was retained. Consequently single aspect apartments were inevitable. In compensation, they were planned as open flowing spaces enjoying the south facing aspect. As the building's use as a nursing home had gutted much of the interior detailing, Davis Duncan Architects gave it their own twist. Kitchen enclosures feature skirting lighting, making these inserted boxes 'float'.

Towers may be striking. However internally they are difficult to convert to residential use. The 'tower' house at Schaw is planned over 3 floors with a further roof terrace which offers one of the finest panoramic views in the city.

Fountainbridge, Edinburgh

WITH THE DECISION BY Scottish and Newcastle to close its operations at Fountainbridge, Edinburgh, a massive development opportunity was presented to transform what had been industrial land to mixed uses more appropriate to the inner city. Most significantly, the sites are bounded by the Union Canal, a vastly neglected resource. The planning authority was anxious to ensure that this featured strongly in any future development proposals and consequently, the City, with the support of S&N as landowners, commissioned a masterplan to secure a cohesive development.

S&N is keen to manage the process effectively, and has allocated the North and West sites to Grosvenor/AMA Developments and the three phases of the south Eastern sites to Buredi – Burrell's joint venture with the City's development arm, EDI.

Edinburgh Quay has already commenced, with greater emphasis on commercial uses rather than residential. The first phase of Buredi's efforts creates a new street – Freer Street – that curves, gently, linking Fountainbridge and the canal. Inevitably, the dynamic planning of triangular blocks met with resistance from some quarters. The majority of the development, and the street, is residential with two new office blocks terminating each terrace as it reaches Fountainbridge. There are also commercial activities at ground floor, canalside, level.

The proposals, with Allan Murray Architects will create a plinth to address car parking and servicing, with the new buildings and the new street constructed above. This massive undertaking allows for a vehicle free street and creates an environment that will link with the canalside environment, and hopefully, a new pedestrian bridge.

Most importantly, was the idea of connecting Bruntsfield with Haymarket, something not possible for decades because of the massive sites former industrial use. This has been aggravated by the construction of the Western Approach Road, as well as the boundary of the canal. The masterplan endeavours to overcome these hurdles.

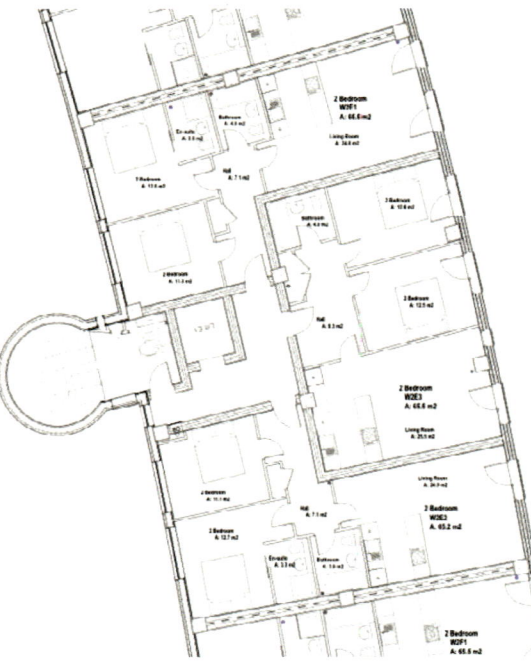

Catalogue

G GLASGOW

1982

1982

1984

1984

3 ST. BERNARD'S ROW, EDINBURGH

This first new-build Kantel design of twenty apartments featured metal balconies on the front façade, then rarely seen in Scottish housing, now commonplace. The building featured in Charles McKean's *Edinburgh Architectural Guide*, where it was described as having "good proportions and post-modern jerky balconies".

WEST CROSSCAUSEWAY/ BUCCLEUCH STREET, EDINBURGH

This enormously successful development was one of Kantel's first, restoring derelict buildings and putting back a mix of uses, primarily residential.

This part of south Edinburgh was, at that time, considered wholly unsuitable for residential use other than student accommodation. This development was the catalyst for a rapid re-evaluation, and a new positive attitude to residential development has resulted in a radical improvement in the whole area.

FORREST HILL, EDINBURGH

These derelict buildings were acquired from the University of Edinburgh for conversion to residential use. This was part of Kantel's early work, when energy was focused on the Old Town of Edinburgh and Glasgow's Merchant City. The internal detailing was crisp and derived heavily from the main restoration theme, with stop-chamfer/timber detailing, a motif repeated in much of Rob Hunter's work.

WEST NICOLSON STREET, EDINBURGH

This development followed on from West Crosscauseway and created student apartments by restoring derelict and dilapidated buildings. The detailing was simple but thorough, restoring wall presses, fireplaces, sash windows and shutters. This approach was almost unheard of for developers at that time.

E 1

E 2

E 3

E 4

Architect	Kantel
Engineer	Blythe & Blythe

Developer	Kantel
Architect	Kantel
QS	Blythe & Blythe
Engineer	Wren & Bell

Developer	Kantel
Architect	Kantel
QS	Blythe & Blythe
Engineer	Wren & Bell

Developer	Kantel
Architect	Kantel
QS	Blythe & Blythe
Engineer	Wren & Bell

1984

1985

1985

1986

EYRE PLACE, EDINBURGH

This design for sheltered housing on a prominent site in Edinburgh's New Town utilised a strong geometry, rather than the pastiche approach which was in vogue at the time. The architect was Eisaku Ushida, who went on to form Ushida Findlay. Kath Findlay was author of our Flagship block at Homes for the Future, fifteen years later.

CALTON ROAD, EDINBURGH

An early Kantel scheme on Calton Road. This involved the conversion of deep-plan redundant warehouses. Well-lit apartments were created by providing an internal light well. The proposals were sited in an area considered at that time totally unsuitable for residential use. The execution was immaculate, interpreting timber details in a robust 'brewery' style. However, to create the aesthetic, the scheme required over twenty relaxations of the building regulations. Across the road, Nick Groves-Raines and John Forbes, through Steinhuis, undertook a development in similar style.

MERCHANT'S LAND, LEITH, EDINBURGH

These unbuilt proposals envisaged a variety of uses overlooking the Shore on the Water of Leith. The buildings were sold on prior to the onset of our first recession. This was unfortunate, as the proposals were of a very high calibre. The new-build, had a delicate touch, entirely appropriate for its context.

CASTLE TERRACE, EDINBURGH

Just at the time of the Burrell demerger with Kantel, these grandiose James Gowans buildings were converted to residential apartments with superb views to Edinburgh Castle. The buildings also housed The Burrell Company's first offices. The detailing to the external restoration is remarkable, including extensive stone repairs and the rebuilding of ornate chimneys.

E 5

E 6

E 7

E 8

Developer	Kantel
Architect	Kantel / Eisaku Ushida

Developer	Kantel
Architect	Kantel / Rob Hunter
QS	Blythe & Blythe
Engineer	Wren & Bell

Developer	Kantel
Architect	Kantel
QS	Blythe & Blythe
Engineer	Blythe & Blythe

Developer	Kantel
Architect	Kantel
QS	Thomson Bethune
Engineer	Wren & Bell

1986

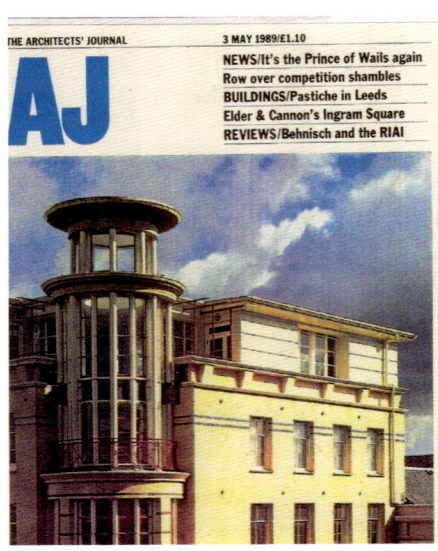

1987

1987

1987

INGRAM SQUARE, GLASGOW

The developer, Yarmadillo, was a joint venture established by Kantel, involving the SDA and the City Council. The Merchant City was not regarded as a residential area at the time that this project was being built and sold. In fact, Ingram Square became the flagship in the regeneration of the Merchant City, providing virtually a complete urban block of housing, both new and refurbished, as well as commercial accommodation. The design was undertaken by Elder & Cannon Architects, their first large commission, commencing a long working relationship with Burrell. Of some considerable significance in the history of regenerating cities, and architecturally a stylish part of Glasgow's drive to be taken seriously in design, this project marked the final act of the original Kantel. Messrs Burrell and Doolan split up during its construction, but jointly ensured that the venture achieved all its high aspirations.

OLD ASSEMBLY CLOSE, EDINBURGH

This early Burrell Company development, on the Royal Mile, involved the restoration of some of the existing fabric forming the closes off the Mile, and converting these properties back to their original residential use.

The proposals also involved the disposal of the former Herriot's Hospital building to the Faculty of Advocates.

New offices for the Festival Fringe were included in the scheme, as was a new home for The Burrell Company. These activities helped rejuvenate the ground floor/ street scene in an otherwise dreary stretch of the Royal Mile – work that was picked up by Buredi some twelve years later.

ROBERTSON'S CLOSE, COWGATE, EDINBURGH

This site, owned by the University of Edinburgh, was ideal for a student housing project providing much needed accommodation. The design exploits the sloping site to supply underground, but naturally vented, car parking spaces for University staff with student flats around a courtyard above the plinth. The scheme, a Post Modern composition, was much heralded in its day. This was the first of many projects that Burrell undertook along the Cowgate corridor of Edinburgh – a much neglected street described by Charles McKean as the 'underbelly' of the Old Town.

FORMER SWIMMING POOL, PORTOBELLO

Edinburgh Council launched an ideas competition to save the Portobello Pool and the regeneration of central Portobello. The proposals reused a 'surplus to requirements' oil rig at the end of a rebuilt pier, and restored the original pool with a new glazed canopy. The Council found this a little too rich and demolished a renowned 1930s lido to create a football pitch.

G 1

E 9

E 10

E 11

Developer	Yarmadillo
Architect	Elder & Cannon Architects
QS	Tozer Gallagher
Engineer	Blythe & Blythe
Graphics	Graven Images

Developer	The Burrell Company
Architect	Simpson & Brown
QS	Reid and Gibson
Engineer	Wren & Bell

Developer	The Burrell Company
Architect	Davis Duncan Architects
QS	Thomson Bethune
Engineer	Wren & Bell

Developer	The Burrell Company
Architect	Nicholas Groves-Raines Architects

1988

1988

1989

1989

DUDDINGSTON NEW-BUILD HOUSING PHASE 1, EDINBURGH

This was the first phase of several projects by Burrell at Duddingston House. Undertaken with Balfour Beatty, the development created a contemporary interpretation of a traditional courtyard in the lea of Duddingston House. Designed by Glasgow-based Simister Monaghan, the project provided a mix of houses and apartments.

Post Modernism is again to the fore, as it was in much work of the period, albeit in a restrained form, and constructed in stone, slate and lead.

The second phase, located well to the south of the House, was never constructed as the recession took hold. The site was eventually taken up by Miller Homes who built their own variation of the design concept.

GARDEN FESTIVAL PAVILION, GLASGOW

This pavilion within a traditional Walled Garden, our contribution to the Festival was a completely 'over the top' exercise in Post Modernism.

The project architect was Keith Cunningham, who went on to do further work for Burrell, most notably Caledon House in Edinburgh in 2002. It was from here that Andy Burrell and John Forbes started their collaboration, Forbes leaving Groves-Raines in 1988.

The model, illustrated, was one of a number of excellent models created by the late Andy Baxter. It hangs on the wall of the Burrell offices to this day.

VICTORIA ROAD, DUNDEE

After several years of work on these proposals to restore a former jute factory in Dundee the scheme lost its way in the provincial politics of Dundee and, regretably, this development did not proceed.

WEST PORT, EDINBURGH

This entire street, leading west out of the Grassmarket, was salvaged from demolition and restored to flats and shops with infill housing to the gap sites.

The project is understated architecturally but represents significant urban regeneration and an important contribution to the townscape.

Edinburgh had lost certain areas of buildings to accommodate 'road improvements'. There were visions of remarkable boldness that almost competed with Glasgow in the civic devastation perpetrated by the Roads Engineer. The reinstatement of areas such as West Port has helped to restore the historic grain of the city.

The development is traditionally configured with ground floor shops and bars, with mixed tenure flats above.

E 12

G 2

E 13

Developer	The Burrell Company
Architect	Simister Monaghan
QS	Thomson Bethune
Engineer	Blythe & Blythe

Developer	The Burrell Company
Architect	Nicholas Groves Raines Architects
Landscape Architect	Peter White

Developer	The Burrell Company
Architect	Simpson & Brown

Developer	The Burrell Company
Architect	PJMP Architects
QS	Thomson Bethune
Engineer	Wren & Bell

1990

WAVERLEY VALLEY, EDINBURGH

This major Scotsman/RIAS sponsored competition sought radical proposals for the regeneration of the Waverley Valley. The Burrell submission, designed with Troughton McAslan Architects, proposed creating a landscaped park, oversailing the railway tracks below.

E 14

Developer   The Burrell Company
Architect   Troughton McAslan Architects
Landscape   Ian White

1990

MORRISON STREET, EDINBURGH

Ted Cullinan Architects designed The Burrell Company/ Argent submission for the architect/developer competition, promoted by the City of Edinburgh to redevelop the Haymarket Goods Yard Sites. Cullinan's plan took much from the layout of the New Town, creating new vistas, streets and crescents.

The proposals were considered by many as the most appropriate for the area, and the opportunity to have a building by Cullinan was a very attractive proposition. Unfortunately the City preferred an alternative submission, which was never built. The site was developed piecemeal.

Having been rejected, Burrell opened a 'Salon des Refuses' in the Royal Mile, which attracted three times the number of visitors as the official exhibition of the chosen design.

E 15

Developer   Argent / The Burrell Company
Architect   Ted Cullinan
QS   Walfords
Engineer   Waterman & Partners

1990

CARRICK QUAY, GLASGOW

One of the most significant residential projects of its day, the designs were the result of a (very) limited competition. Four firms were invited to submit ideas for the redevelopment of this riverside site and Davis Duncan Architects submitted the preferred design.

The site overlooks the River Clyde and at one time the SV Carrick (the world's oldest colonial clipper), which was unfortunately 'moved on' after the project was underway.

The area around the former Briggait market – the location of the site – was extremely run down and this development was one of the forerunners to major riverside development. The timing of the project was unfortunate in that the recession had a major effect upon the housing market. The withdrawal of a Scottish Development Agency grant at the eleventh hour was also unhelpful.

G 3

Developer   The Burrell Company and Balfour Beatty
Architect   Davis Duncan Architects
QS   Thomas & Adamson
Engineer   Barclay Dowds

1991

FETTES VILLAGE, EDINBURGH

Lilley Developments formed a joint venture with Burrell to pursue major mixed use projects in Scotland. With the might of the Lilley balance sheet, and the vision and local knowledge of Burrell, the Company seemed destined for great things. Alas collapse followed Lilley's bankruptcy in London. The effect upon Burrell was catastrophic, but not fatal.

Fettes Village was half built when the company ceased trading. A scheme of flats, houses and a leisure centre, the original plan had been designed by retirement home developers, McCarthy and Stone, who sold the site on having started the foundations.

The aesthetic was reviewed as were the internal plans. Davis Duncan Architects were retained to carry out the work. Ultimately half of the scheme was undertaken by another developer to a significantly cheaper specification.

E 16

Developer   Fettes Village Ltd
   (Lilley Developments and The
   Burrell Company)
Architect   Davis Duncan Architects
QS   Thomson Bethune

1991

1992

1992

1992

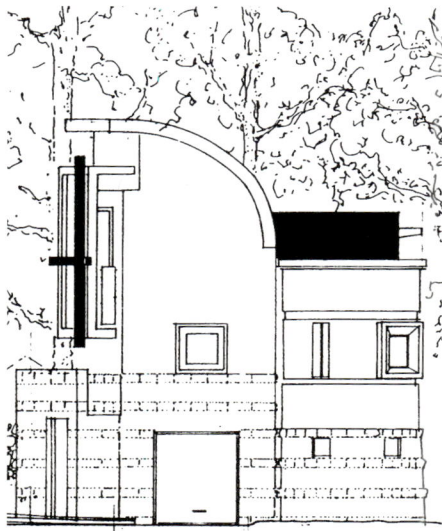

TOLLCROSS, EDINBURGH

The second development site owned by Burrell/Lilleys was the former SMT Triangle at Tollcross. Unlike Fettes, no site start was made here, primarily due to the City's legal department failing to issue a Section 75 Agreement.

The project would have created new street frontages with new, tenemental style, properties concealing a multi-storey car park behind. The proposal included flats for the local housing association (an early example of the 'Affordable Housing Policy'), a health centre, shops, offices and flats for sale.

BLACKFRIARS STREET, EDINBURGH

This unbuilt proposal for a gap site in Edinburgh's Old Town won the Royal Scottish Academy's gold medal in the summer exhibition of 1992. The designs, by Elder & Cannon, proposed residential apartments over ground floor commercial but retained, as required in the purchase, a pend access to the multi-storey carpark owned by the Scandic Crown Hotel.

With the economic recession the vendor was bankrupted and the purchase did not proceed. This was unfortunate, as it would have been the first Edinburgh job for Elder & Cannon. Burrell were keen to shake up the Edinburgh establishment, dragging the design aspirationists to a higher level, and felt it needed a Glasgow firm to set the standard. It wasn't until Upper Strand in 2005 that Elder & Cannon finally built in the east for Burrell.

DUDDINGSTON HOUSE, EDINBURGH

This stunning set piece was designed by Sir William Chambers for the Duke of Abercorn. The enormous double height entrance lobby was reputedly designed to allow the Duke to ride his horse into the hallway and then dismount.

By the late twentieth century the building had become a rather forlorn motel. Apart from the seedy nature of its presentation, the building was in serious need of repair and restoration. After its acquisition by Burrell we determined to keep the property in a single use, preferably an upmarket hotel. The market was not propitious and the building sat vacant for some time until it was converted into offices and then sold to a neighbouring firm of architects who made it their head office.

A programme of repairs was undertaken to salvage the property, including the restoration of some of Chambers' detailing.

FETTES LODGE COMPETITION, EDINBURGH

This was the first national open architectural competition organised by the Company (in tandem with the Royal Incorporation of Architects in Scotland). The site was located at the entrance to the driveway leading to the development site. The idea was to create a lodge that would announce the entrance to Fettes Village.

The entries were in the hundreds – the Fruitmarket Gallery had to be hired to house all of the submissions. The range of architectural solutions was staggering and the judges, chaired by Professor Metzstein, selected the above design. Unfortunately, the proposed design suffered as, like much of the rest of the project, it was never built.

E 17

E 18

E 19

E 20

Developer   Tollcross Dev Ltd
              (The Burrell Company and
              Lilley Developments Ltd)
Architect   Campbell & Arnott Architects
QS   Thomson Bethune
Engineer   Blythe & Blythe

Developer   The Burrell Company
Architect   Elder & Cannon Architects
QS   Summers & Partners
Engineer   David Narro Associates

Developer   The Burrell Company
Architect   The Burrell Company
QS   Thomson Bethune
Engineer   David Narro Associates

Developer   The Burrell Company
Architect   David Miller

1992

1992

1992

1993

FETTES VILLAGE LEISURE CENTRE, EDINBURGH

As part of the village our idea was to create a small leisure centre which would house a swimming pool, gym, snooker room and changing facilities, as well as a bar and restaurant. There would be outdoor tennis courts built above a new, carefully concealed car park for the development.

A second phase envisaged a bowling green on a further car park structure. Initially the idea was to make the leisure facilities solely for use by the purchasers of the flats, but this proved financially unsound. Regrettably, after ten years another developer acquired the leisure buildings, levelled the lot and redeveloped the site for flats!

GLASGOW TOWER COMPETITION

Burrell organised the largest ever international competition for a Scottish site from an idea developed with Stuart Gulliver, Chief Executive of Scottish Enterprise Glasgow (then the GDA) to promote design opportunities and excellence in Glasgow, and to provide the city with an iconic structure – Glasgow's own Eiffel Tower.

The competition was enormously successful with entrants from all over the world, and a strong submission from Europe.

An eminent judging panel was led by Sir Norman Foster alongside Tony Hunt and David Mackay.

The winning design, by Richard Horden, was finally built, on a new site to the south of the Clyde.

CROWN STREET, GORBALS SUBMISSION, GLASGOW
PHASE 1

Promoted as the IBA of Glasgow, the first phase development of Piers Gough's masterplan was promoted as a major 'development opportunity'. Burrell cleared with the promoters that using CZWG would be acceptable, and duly prepared a submission.

The judges dismissed the scheme as "…too architectural…" which, regrettably, set the tone for the first phases of the Crown Street regeneration. Happily, as the regeneration of the area has progressed, its architecture has become much more 'architectural' – clearly those now responsible have a great deal more confidence than their predecessors. In fact, the most recent phase of the Gorbals Regeneration includes a major CZWG building.

18 WOODSIDE TERRACE, GLASGOW

The company decided to diversify, and acquired this townhouse as an office upgrade. A simple conversion and certainly not up there with Burrell's greatest hits.

The completion of the office conversion was launched timeously to coincide with an all-time low in the commercial property market.

This first time entry into pure commercial property development for Burrell became the last for some time.

E 21

G 4

G 5

G 6

Developer   The Burrell Company
Architect   Davis Duncan Architects
QS   Thomson Bethune

Competition The Burrell Company / GDA
Architect   Richard Horden Architects

Developer   The Burrell Company
Architect   CZWG Architects

Developer   The Burrell Company
Architects   Bamber Gray
QS   Reid Associates
Engineer   Patterson Associates

1993

DUDDINGSTON HOUSE COURTYARD, EDINBURGH

The original stables and servants' courtyard designed by Sir William Chambers includes a chapel (previously converted to apartments by others) as its centrepiece. These buildings were in serious disrepair, the west wing being roofless. Burrell set about creating six individual houses.

Although plans were prepared for the development as a whole, each house was redesigned internally to suit the requirements of its new owner. Consequently plan types vary from the more traditional, to split level and open plan. Externally the property was fully restored, with the east facing arched doorways being glazed and the original doorways retained as 'shutters'.

E 22

Developer	The Burrell Company
Architect	The Burrell Company
QS	Thomson Bethune
Engineer	David Narro Associates

1994

NAPIER ROAD, MERCHISTON, EDINBURGH

Burrell struggled to rebuild its portfolio following the recession. This little project on Napier Road drew upon recent experiences, particularly at Duddingston House Courtyard, with its houses designed to particular clients' requirements. The villa had a coach house, which became one home, the remainder being converted to three units.

At the time of writing, all of the original purchasers were in occupation, which is unusual in Edinburgh. The principal house was sold to a colleague with whom Burrell would forge the Premier Burrell joint venture some ten years later.

E 23

Developer	The Burrell Company
Architect	The Burrell Company
QS	Thomson Bethune
Engineer	David Narro Associates

1994

DEAN VILLAGE, EDINBURGH

Another small refurb and new-build on an extremely tight site in Dean Village followed the Napier Road project. The existing building was in some state of decay.

Burrell's proposals provided three apartments in the restored building, but also added two new houses in a more contemporary style. The small but dynamic spaces were topped by a roof in terne-coated steel, differentiating this from the restored property. The scheme was popular, and helped Burrell get back on its feet.

E 24

Developer	The Burrell Company
Architect	Adam Dudley Associates
QS	Thomson Bethune
Engineer	David Narro Associates

1994

RONALDSON'S WHARF, EDINBURGH

Like Coalhill, which Buredi did some six years later, this key site, beside the Water of Leith, was included in Edinburgh's bid for the designation 'City of Architecture and Design 1999'.

The idea was to hold a three stage architect/developer competition, the first being an open architectural competition, the second stage inviting five firms to develop their ideas further, with the third open to developers to acquire the site on the basis of building the chosen design.

Burrell 'designed' the procurement route, managed the competition and monitored the process through to completion.

E 25

Developer	Miller / Crudens
Architect	Fraser Brown McKenna in association with Dignan Reed & Dewar

1994

1995

1995

1995

THE PIPING CENTRE, GLASGOW

Glasgow's Planning Department encouraged Burrell to save this elegant little neo-classical building which was under severe threat. Building Control was looking to have the property 'made safe', all too often a euphemism for demolition.

Early ideas were along the usual lines of offices over a bar/restaurant, but through a timely act of nepotism, it transpired that the Scottish Piping fraternity needed a home.

Burrell assisted in establishing a Trust, negotiated grants, and transferred the property, assisting in managing the project to completion.

It has quickly become a world-class Centre of Piping.

BRUNSWICK ROAD, EDINBURGH

A relatively simple new-build development undertaken by Burrell as a turnkey for Link Housing Association. The scheme involved the acquisition of the site, procuring the development, through to the final project completion.

TAILORS' HALL, EDINBURGH

For years Burrell had sought to acquire this superb but derelict 'A' listed property in the Cowgate. Various schemes were proposed but the solution which was adopted incorporated the restoration of the external building and courtyard, with the internal fit-out being the responsibility of the purchaser – in this case a bar/hotel operator.

The reuse of this property had a very positive effect upon the regeneration of the Cowgate, formerly one of the seedier streets in the city.

Much earlier, Burrell had identified the opportunity for further student housing on the adjacent site to satisfy the demands of the University. It took many years to deliver the overall package.

THE HOLYROOD STUDY, EDINBURGH

Burrell was invited by Lothian and Edinburgh Enterprise Limited to review the development proposals for the sites to the south east of the Royal Mile. An overly ambitious architectural proposal, prepared by an Edinburgh practice on behalf of Scottish Enterprise, could not be implemented, particularly at a time when the recession had taken the construction industry to a record low.

Burrell retained Richard Reid Architect and developed a plan that reflected the historic street fishbone pattern of the Old Town, identifying sites for 'major commercial/cultural use'. The proposal included the relocation of the Scottish and Newcastle brewery and the re-use of this site for leisure. LEEL then promoted the plan, seeking developer agents to implement the proposals.

Eventually the study information was applied to the selection of the site for the new Scottish Parliament. The implementation of Burrell's initial proposals were taken forward by others.

G 7

E 26

E 27

E 28

Developer	The Piping Trust
Architects	McGurn Logan Duncan & Opfer Architects
Museum Design	Lee Boyd Architects
QS	KLM Partnership
M&E	Henderson Warnock

Developer	The Burrell Company
Architect	Keith Cunningham Architects
QS	Ross & Morton
Engineer	Robertson Eadie

Developer	The Burrell Company
Architect	Davis Duncan Architects
QS	Ross & Morton
Engineer	Harley Haddow

Consultant	The Burrell Company
Architect	Richard Reid

1996

1996

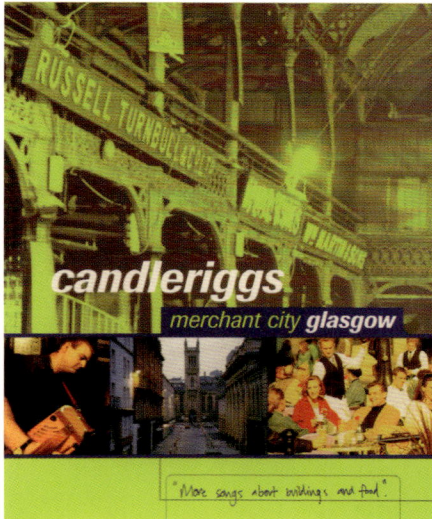

1997

1997

RAMSAY GARDEN, EDINBURGH

This magnificent composition sits in the lee of Edinburgh Castle. A large part of the development had been taken over by a bank as a training centre. Burrell acquired the property and set about restoring it to residential use – Sir Patrick Geddes' original intention.

The buildings had been much altered, and the conversion to create flats and houses was challenging to say the least. Structural problems emerged as the buildings were opened up – with floor spans that defied most building codes – and gravity! Happily it's now quite safe – and remains one of Edinburgh's most desirable addresses.

CITY HALLS, GLASGOW

It was proposed to refurbish the City Halls by incorporating neighbouring sites and cross-funding developments. The plans were very much in line with the city's ambitions at that time. Unfortunately, personnel changes in the Council meant that the proposals would remain largely unbuilt.

The idea was eventually promoted – without a developer – although the adjacent site remains vacant some ten years later.

CLEVEDEN DRIVE, GLASGOW

Glasgow's West End contains some of the finest Victorian villas in Scotland. Two such buildings were redeveloped as a series of elegant apartments through the removal of latter day accretions, and the restoration of detail to return the buildings to their original appearance.

ST PANCRAS, LONDON

In this national architect/developer competition, The Burrell Company was shortlisted with two of the most significant development companies in the country. Although not selected, the competition signalled that The Burrell Company was capable of making its mark outwith Scotland in urban regeneration.

E 29

G 8

Developer	The Burrell Company
Architect	The Burrell Company
QS	Thomson Bethune
Engineer	David Narro Associates

Developer	The Burrell Company
Architect	Davis Duncan Architects

Developer	The Burrell Company
Architect	CRGP
QS	CRGP
Engineer	Waterman Rennick

Developer	The Burrell Company
Architect	John McAslan

1997

1998

1998

1998

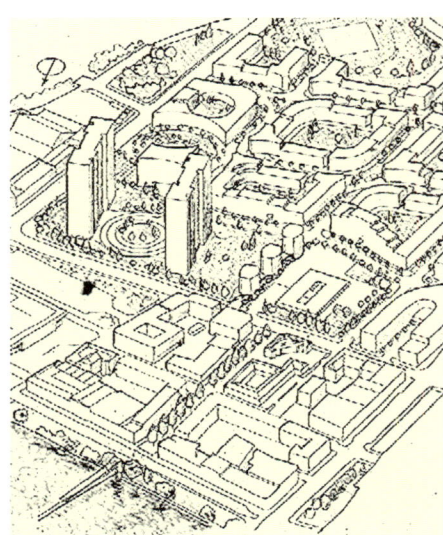

THE PARK, GLASGOW

Park School was acquired for conversion into flats. It was the first development at this scale to endorse Glasgow's City Plan policy to return the Park area to housing, its original use under Charles Wilson's late nineteenth century plan for the area.

The series of townhouses were linked internally to suit the previous use as a girls' school. This made the restoration and conversion to apartments a little awkward, as did the steel framework which provided the buildings' internal structure – however, this challenge was overcome to provide superb contemporary apartment spaces, rich in period detail.

BARTHOLOMEW HOUSE, EDINBURGH

Formerly the offices of the renowned mapmaker and home to the National Geographic Society, this fine 'B' listed building became surplus to requirements and was converted to five apartments.

Design was undertaken in-house, and involved liaison with potential purchasers to create highly individual apartments, including one of Scotland's earliest loft conversions.

FOUNTAINBRIDGE LIBRARY, EDINBURGH

One left over from the recession when Burrell undertook various activities just to stay alive, including the refurbishment of the City of Edinburgh's Fountainbridge Library.

It created accommodation for the Citizens Advice Bureau within the vacant top floor whilst refurbishing circulation and other accommodation for the Book Festival.

NEW LAURIESTON, GLASGOW

Proposals undertaken by Burrell, EDI and Miller foresaw major opportunities in this largely derelict area, formerly Glasgow's Gorbals. Proposals were drafted by Piers Gough, CZWG, following his award-winning masterplan for neighbouring Crown Street.

The Company acquired several sites within the area. The majority of other sites were owned by the Council, which steadfastly blocked every proposal to take forward the regeneration exercise for almost ten years. Ultimately they agreed to new proposals being commissioned by the Crown Street team.

G 9

E 30

E 31

G 10

Developer	The Burrell Company
Architect	Davis Duncan Architects
QS	Ross & Morton

Developer	The Burrell Company
Architect	The Burrell Company
QS	Thomson Bethune
Engineer	David Narro Associates

Developer	The Burrell Consultancy
Architect	Keith Cunningham Architects
QS	SRC
Engineer	David Narro Associates

Developer	The Burrell Company / EDI / Miller
Architect	CZWG Architects

1998

1999

1999

2000

SMYLLUM HOUSE, LANARK

By the time Burrell acquired the site, there was very little left of Smyllum House. The main façade and tower, with parts of the elevations, were all that survived. The building was rebuilt, and five apartments created. The site was part of a larger development, with six new-build townhouses constructed to the rear to subsidise the rebuilding of Smyllum House itself.

The designs of the courtyard houses were contemporary, elegantly and skilfully designed by the talented architect Lucy Parr, who sadly died before the project was complete.

DUBLIN COLONIES, EDINBURGH

EDI was struggling to make sense out of the competition-winning design for the Colonies site, by Richard Murphy, and invited Burrell to have a look. Burrell refined the scheme by removing some garages and covered car parking spaces, and also proposed the demolition of a non-descript brick warehouse building to allow for houses, thereby offering a mix of accommodation types.

Although hampered by the very poor performance of the contractor (the scheme was one year late on a one year programme), the project was a huge success, winning an RIBA Award in 2000. This was the first Buredi project.

HOMES FOR THE FUTURE, GLASGOW

Glasgow City of Architecture and Design 1999 had the Homes for the Future project as its flagship. Developers were requested to select an architect from each of three lists – local, national and international – and then to submit proposals for consideration. The winners would build their schemes as part of the 1999 Expo.

Burrell won three blocks – two with McKeown Alexander Architects, and one with Ushida Findlay Architects. The Ushida Findlay plan created a narrow building (overlooking Glasgow Green with deep, curving balconies on its rear, northward elevation). McKeown Alexander created two schemes, one a terrace of townhouses, the other an 'object building'.

Happily the Ushida Findlay building has become an iconic image of Glasgow featuring in tourist literature and numerous press articles about the city's architectural renaissance.

COALHILL, EDINBURGH

Buredi's second project, again started as an architectural competition – this being part of the Edinburgh bid for City of Architecture and Design in 1999.

The idea was for three 'home' firms and three 'away' firms to submit ideas for development. The design selected was by Allan Murray Architects – ironically the only Edinburgh practice.

Poor cost advice resulted in several significant 'refinements' being required prior to the scheme getting underway. The buildings were voted 'The Best Apartment Block in the UK' in 2001.

E 32

G 11

E 33

Developer	The Burrell Company
Architect	Parr Shearer
QS	CRGP
Engineer	Waterman Rennick

Developer	Dublin Street Devs Ltd (Buredi)
Architect	Richard Murphy Architects
QS	Ross & Morton
Engineer	Robertson Eadie

Developer	The Burrell Company
Architects	Ushida Findlay / McKeown Alexander
QS	KLM Partnership
Engineer	Ove Arup & Partners

Developer	Buredi
Architect	Allan Murray Architects
QS	Ross & Morton
Engineer	Ove Arup & Partners

2000

2000

2001

2001

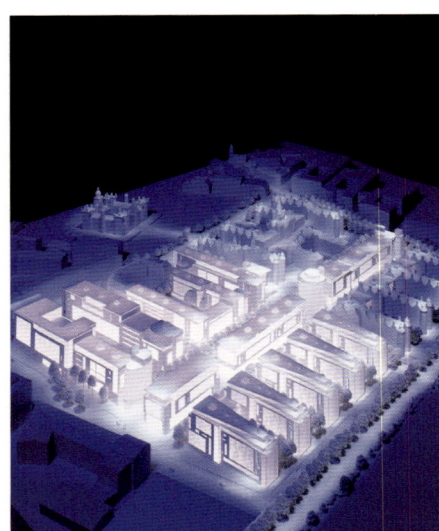

EDINBURGH PARK COMPETITION

Burrell was invited by Edinburgh Park Limited to organise a design competition for an office site. The winners were Campbell & Arnott Architects.

THE CHAMBERS, EDINBURGH

This conversion of the former dental hospital on Edinburgh's Chambers Street generated a mix of uses including apartments, offices for the National Museums of Scotland and a restaurant and bar. A tortuous plan arrangement meant much internal remodelling, not least to satisfy the requirements of the proposed new mix of uses.

56 BELFORD ROAD, EDINBURGH

This tight corner site in the West End gave Richard Murphy an opportunity to create a corner building which terminated the street, but also dropped height drastically to address the scale of the mews properties behind.

The original design was regrettably, too rich for the Planning Officers, who insisted on shaving off the top corner, resulting in a less elegant solution. Notwithstanding, the scheme remains full of little delights – the central stair is in fact an 'outside space' capped by a tent!

The views from the penthouse apartment across to Fife are exceptional.

FORMER ROYAL INFIRMARY, EDINBURGH

Burrell and EDI, with Morrisons, produced an ambitious and exciting scheme for the architect/developer competition for the regeneration of this strategically important site. A scheme by Foster Associates won the day. The Health Trust, as landowner, had a surprising late and unfortunate change of heart. Regrettably, another architectural gem – in this case from Murray's office – was lost, but the winning design has justly recognised the importance of this site.

E 34

E 35

E 36

Development The Burrell Company
Consultant
Architect   Campbell & Arnott Architects

Developer   The Burrell Company / Morrisons
Architect   Lee Boyd Architects
QS   Ross and Morton
Engineer   Will Rudd Associates

Developer   Buredi
Architect   Richard Murphy Architects
QS   Summers Inman
Engineer   Robertson Eadie

Developer   Burrell / EDI / Morrisons
Architect   Allan Murray Architects

2001

LEITH HOUSE, EDINBURGH

As part of the overall regeneration of Coalhill, this formerly derelict building, adjacent to the Coalhill site, was acquired and refurbished to provide accommodation for the homeless and rough sleepers.

The development was undertaken by Dunedin Housing Association as part of the overall area regeneration by Buredi.

E 37

Developer Buredi / Dunedin Housing Association
Architect Lee Boyd Architects

2001

NO. 1 PARLIAMENT SQUARE, EDINBURGH

In itself an interesting conversion but, more importantly, the scheme marked the first phase of what was the Tron Regeneration Project.

The buildings housed Police and Social Work, and the District Courts. However, they were poorly planned and, after we had remodelled the Courts, the remaining space was converted to apartments, restaurants and offices.

These new uses animate the street, particularly the top of Old Fishmarket Close, which runs through the Tron regeneration area.

E 38

Developer Buredi
Architects Jenkins & Marr
QS Armour & Partners
Engineer Will Rudd Associates

2002

CALEDON HOUSE, EDINBURGH

New-build housing on an infill site in Edinburgh, this simple block of fourteen apartments was much inspired by Scandinavian design and their utilisation of mature, tree-covered sites.

Sustainability was a principal issue in the design, and this is demonstrated, both in the building's appearance and its performance.

However, it is for media hype and a confrontation with Edinburgh's planning authority that this project will be most remembered. Ironically, when Burrell moved the building a few feet to save existing trees, a neighbour managed to stir up a frenzy of misinformation, intent on getting it demolished. Happily, his assertion that the building sat too close to his own was erroneous and matters were eventually resolved.

E 39

Developer The Burrell Company
Architect Keith Cunningham Architects
QS CRGP
Engineer Waterman Rennick

2002-

BANGOUR VILLAGE, WEST LOTHIAN

Bangour Village was a hospital near Livingston which became surplus to requirements. Proposals by Burrell and Persimmon to regenerate the area were selected as the preferred bid by the Hospital Trust.

Burrell's role is to restore the majority of the 'A' listed buildings, converting them to apartments and houses. The project also involves devising alternative uses for some of the major public buildings, including the church.

Developer The Burrell Company / Persimmon Homes
Architect The Burrell Company
QS Thomson Bethune

2002

2003

2003

2004

TRON NURSERY, EDINBURGH

The Tron Square competition judges decided that the new nursery building be awarded to Allan Murray Architects. The original Cowgate Nursery had its play area directly beside the most polluted road in the Old Town. Re-siting the nursery was key to the Tron regeneration proposals.

Initially there was considerable resistance to the proposals, most absurdly from the Faculty of Advocates, who objected to the new location of the nusery school on the basis that little children are noisy. However, logic prevailed and the innovative nursery design was created away from the danger and pollution of the main road – a victory for good sense.

OTAGO STREET, GLASGOW

Although unbuilt, this remarkable proposal promoted a significant urban intervention in Glasgow's West End. The residential block on a partially vacant site on Otago Street ran into legal complications with neighbouring landowners and, as a consequence, the project did not proceed.

TRON, EDINBURGH

The site for this competition-winning, Richard Murphy scheme, a multi-storey car park for Council officials and councillors, was demolished to make way for this mixed use development.

The two new buildings flank a reinstated close which, symbolically, arrives at the door of the architect's own office. A key component to the regeneration of the Tron Square area, the lower floors accommodate commercial activities, including a restaurant opening out onto a small terrace on Fishmarket Close.

112 WEST BOW, EDINBURGH
(FORMER TRAVERSE THEATRE)

These buildings were in a derelict condition. Burrell sought to keep these properties in the public realm – indeed a Planning Consent was granted for hotel use. However, the Council were concerned over the introduction of more licensed premises in the Old Town. As a consequence, the scheme was redesigned as apartments.

Although extremely successful, this is a lost opportunity for the city. Perhaps the councillors concerned did not fully appreciate the potential benefits of what could have been a marvellous, European quality, public usage – just imagine the gentle delights of sipping an espresso in an off-street square as the sharp sunlight of an early autumnal day reflects off the elegantly restored stone façades of the new Traverse Hotel. Ah well…

E 40

E 41

E 42

Developer	Buredi and CRHA
Architect	Allan Murray Architects
QS	Ross and Morton
Engineer	Will Rudd Associates

Developer	The Burrell Company
Architect	RMJM Architects
QS	Armour & Partners
Engineer	RMJM Architects

Developer	Buredi
Architect	Richard Murphy Architects
QS	Ross & Morton
Engineer	David Narro Associates

Developer	Buredi
Architect	Lee Boyd Architects
QS	Summerfield Robb Clark Ltd
Engineer	Jim McColl Associates

2004

GREYFRIARS HOSTEL CONVERSION, EDINBURGH

Formerly an unsuitable and cramped hostel for homeless people, the conversion of this cellular narrow section building to apartments posed a real challenge. A brand new homeless facility had been built at Leith House.

The poorly built rear extensions to the building were demolished to create a courtyard space that relates to the conversion of the former Traverse Theatre.

Officers in the city's Housing Department were convinced that the nature of the construction rendered this particular building unconvertable.

E 43

Developer   Buredi
Architect   Lee Boyd Architects
QS   Summerfield Robb Clark Ltd
Engineer   Jim McColl Associates

2004

PORTOBELLO, EDINBURGH

The overall masterplanning proposals to regenerate Portobello were produced by Buredi but, sadly, without full co-operation from the City of Edinburgh Council which was required to take the concept forward. Key sites were sold off by the Estates Department which meant that this vision could not be pursued.

E 44

Developer   Buredi
Architect   Allan Murray Architects

2004

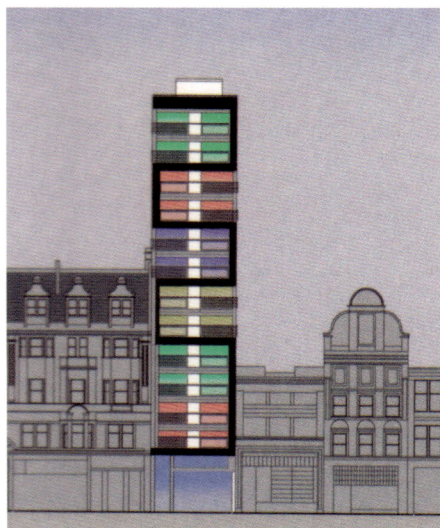

SAUCHIEHALL STREET, GLASGOW

This bold unbuilt submission for the redevelopment of a small site at the western extremity of Sauchiehall Street proposed the creation of 'micro' apartments, stacked high, overlooking Sauchiehall Street. This development proposal, surprisingly, was not favoured by the City Council.

G 12

Developer   The Burrell Company
Architect   Kinnear & Crotch Architects

2004-

UPPER STRAND, EDINBURGH

A dynamic contribution to the overall masterplan of Edinburgh's waterfront at Granton. This architect/ developer competition-winning scheme for 500 apartments is a joint venture with the Places for People Group. The project's first phase is the flagship of the Waterfront. The scheme is organised around a new public square and creates a signal tower block – a landmark within the new townscape proposals.

E 45

Developer   Upper Strand Developments Ltd
Architect   Elder & Cannon Architects / Reiach & Hall Architects
QS   Mackenzie Partnership
Engineer   Cundall Johnston & Partners

2005-

2005-

2005-

2005

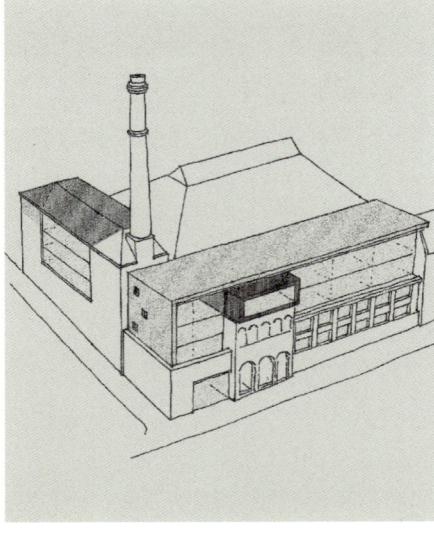

INFIRMARY STREET, EDINBURGH

This derelict former swimming baths was under threat of demolition. Buredi's proposal was to create artists' accommodation in the main swimming pool area and to cross-fund this exercise by a residential development, utilising the remainder of the site, including the ruined former ladies bathing area. The Council liked the idea so, after four years of effort, they sold it to one of our prospective 'tenants'.

MADELVIC, EDINBURGH

Part of the Waterfront Edinburgh Regeneration. What had been the original (short lived) Madelvic Car Factory was derelict. However, the building has historical significance, and was retained as part of the development to provide apartments, sheltered housing, commercial accommodation and live/work units

The project overlooks the new boulevard running diagonally through the development sites to the shore. The buildings are of a 'metropolitan' scale and have a harder face to the street, with a softer, south facing, courtyard side. This enables the creation of dual aspect apartments with access galleries doubling as sun spaces.

MOUNT ZION CHURCH, QUARRIERS VILLAGE

The proposals for the conversion of this huge, redundant church to residential use were highly sensitive. The scheme went to appeal and was finally approved the following year. The designs, by RMJM Architects, create a dynamic intervention in a very sensitive enclosure. Many of the original features of the church are fully retained with apartments enjoying rose windows, rich stone columns and wonderful timber trusses. Each of the twelve apartments created is, as one would expect, unique.

It is proposed to enhance this development with the conversion of the former village clothing shop and adjacent villa to form residential units. A complementary new-build development fronts the local burn. This infill exercise brings more permanent residents to this beautiful Victorian planned village to the west of Glasgow.

RAVELRIG HOUSE, EDINBURGH

This was the first scheme by Premier Burrell to be completed. Ravelrig House and Stables were restored with five new homes in the stables courtyard, and six in the house itself. The project was made more difficult by the fact that the house was burned down the day before it was to be acquired by the company!

The designs incorporated elements of the refurbished buildings coupled with contemporary additions. The designs for the house became more new than old, following the fire. The original planning application was done jointly with Bryant Homes – its interest being the building of new houses in the extensive grounds of Ravelrig House.

E 46

E 47

Developer	Buredi
Architect	Gareth Hoskins
QS	Summerfield Robb Clark
Engineer	W.A. Fairhurst & Partners

Developer	Buredi
Architect	Malcolm Fraser Architects
QS	Summerfield Robb Clark
Engineer	Ove Arup & Partners

Developer	The Burrell Company
Architect	RMJM Architects
QS	CRGP

Developer	Premier Burrell Ltd
Architect	Gareth Hoskins Architects
QS	Summerfield Robb Clark Ltd
Engineer	Cundall Johnston & Partners

2005   2005-   2005-   2005-

CITY HOSPITAL, ABERDEEN

After some considerable time chasing development opportunities in Aberdeen, Burrell emerged with two projects, the first of which was the conversion of the City Hospital to apartments and houses.

Located in a poor area of the city, this regeneration exercise has been well received, and the usual Burrell approach, of retaining as much as possible of the original properties to create bright, open apartments, yielded a positive first project in the north-east. The intial planning application was made jointly with Stewart Milne Homes, Premier Burrell undertaking all the conversion projects with Stewart Milne delivering its own house types thereafter.

BELL'S MILLS, EDINBURGH

Set on the Water of Leith in Edinburgh's West End, this development site, adjacent to an existing hotel, provides twenty-four apartments in three separate blocks arranged in an organic fashion, over underground car parking.

The original, stone-built, Bell's Mill Miller's House, dating from the early nineteenth century, is restored as a single dwelling.

The new-build accommodation was designed with views primarily to the south, overlooking the Water of Leith. The buildings were 'hoisted' to a height well in excess of the 200 year flood level and particular attention was paid to aspects around the site, in particular built-in underground crawl-ways for badgers.

COALHILL II, EDINBURGH

Following the success of Coalhill, a number of further initiatives were promoted by Buredi in the immediate area.

This second phase of the Coalhill development accommodates some housing for Dunedin Housing Association, but the bulk of the development is apartments for sale. The courtyard style plan is built over semi-underground car parking. The majority of the apartments command superb views over the Water of Leith.

As part of the proposals, the neighbouring greenspace was redesigned as a play park. A small urban square is also envisaged to link the 'gable ends' of all the Coalhill projects.

VIENNA APARTMENTS, GLASGOW

An incredible amount of floor space 'over the shop' is vacant in central Glasgow. This proposal involves both the refurbishment of an existing building set between Mitchell Street and Union Street and a new-build block opposite the Lighthouse. The proposals create apartments of various sizes, retaining commercial uses at ground floor and basement level.

The name 'Vienna Apartments' derives from the Secessionist impression created by the internal glazed courtyards as the building snakes through the urban block from one street to the other.

E 48   E 49   G 13

Developer	Premier Burrell Ltd / Stewart Milne Homes
Architect	David Murray Associates Ltd
QS	Murray Montgomery Partnership
Engineer	W. A. Fairhurst & Partners

Developer	Buredi / Bishop Loch
Architects	Farningham McCreadie Partnership
QS	Summerfield Robb Clark Ltd
Engineer	W. A. Fairhurst & Partners

Developer	Buredi
Architect	Allan Murray Architects
QS	Summerfield Robb Clark Ltd
Engineer	Faber Maunsell

Developer	Premier Burrell Ltd
Architect	GM+AD Architects
QS	Thomas & Adamson
Engineer	Woolgar Hunter
M&E	DSSR

2005-   2005-   2006   2006-

FREER STREET, EDINBURGH

With the closure of Scottish & Newcastle Breweries, a major tract of inner city land became available for redevelopment. S&N created a masterplan which was then partially allocated, following negotiation, to Buredi.

The first phase of the Buredi proposals, near Freer Street, offered Allan Murray Architects the rare opportunity to create a new street within the inner city of Edinburgh.

The gently curving street, linking the canal with Fountainbridge, will also open up routes through the city. This permeability is a key component in the regeneration of the area, much sought after by Edinburgh's planning authority. This first phase is 180 houses with two large office blocks and other commercial and retail activities.

MURRAY'S MILLS, MANCHESTER

The first Burrell project to be built south of the border is the regeneration of an amazing courtyard of listed buildings. Dating from 1798-1806, the existing buildings required a complete programme of restoration costing in excess of £11m.

These properties, part of the regeneration of Ancoats, will be converted internally to provide over 100 apartments and commercial accommodation. A new hotel is also part of the overall proposals.

ELMHILL HOUSE, ABERDEEN

This distinctive neo-classical building, previously a hospital, was reputedly severely bomb-damaged in the Second World War. Burrell set about rebuilding the areas damaged by the bombing, and restoring and converting the property to apartments.

This project was a joint planning application with Stewart Milne Homes, with Burrell undertaking the restoration project. The setting of Elmhill House is splendid.

ASSEMBLY STREET, EDINBURGH

This proposal retains a small, listed warehouse for conversion whilst clearing the former industrial premises to create a site for new-build, first time buyer, homes – desperately required in Edinburgh.

Sutherland Hussey's designs propose striking, simple modern housing clustered around an intimate courtyard. These 'cheap' apartments are designed to be delightfully bright and, although small, superbly well detailed.

E 50   E 51

Developer	Buredi
Architect	Allan Murray Architects
QS	David Adamson
Engineer	Faber Maunsell

Developer	The Burrell Company / Inpartnership
Architect	Richard Murphy Architects
QS	Gardiner and Theobold
Engineer	Ove Arup & Partners

Developer	Premier Burrell Ltd
Architect	David Murray
QS	Murray Montgomery & Partners
Engineer	W. A. Fairhurst & Partners

Developer	The Burrell Company
Architect	Sutherland Hussey Architects
QS	Thomson Bethune
Engineer	Harley Haddow

2006-   2006-   2006   2006-

GORTON MONASTERY, MANCHESTER

This competition proposal created a mix of visitor centre, commercial, live-work units and residential accommodation completing a cloister to the St. Francis Church and Monastery and creating a further adjacent cloister (as originally conceived by Edward Pugin).

Although unapologetically 'modern' the proposed materials are 'traditional' – red and blue brick, and Derbyshire stone.

HAWKHEAD, PAISLEY

For his native Paisley, Thomas Tait designed the Infectious Diseases Hospital which, in its axial layout, and in the Deco infused modernity of its various pavilions, was a bold precedent in terms of the planning and design approach to the Glasgow Empire Exhibition that followed in 1938. Undoubtedly one of the most significant and innovative architects of his era, Tait had already worked on the Royal Masonic Hospital at Ravenscourt Park, London. This experience is reflected in both the style of the Paisley Hospital and in the uncluttered design of the buildings' internal spaces.

The setting at Hawkhead, like many hospitals of its era, is an attractive parkland environment. The historic importance of this development relies on the setting, grouping and external appearance of the buildings; their relatively plain interiors lend themselves well to residential adaptation.

DRUMSHEUGH GARDENS, EDINBURGH

These three Victorian town houses in the West End had been much altered to create a temporary hospital and, latterly, a nursing home. Following the closure of the home they were acquired by Premier Burrell for restoration to residential use. 21 apartments of varying sizes and styles have been created, taking advantage of some of the alteration work that had happened in the history of the buildings, most notably the installation of lift access and the large areas of glazing to the rear of the property – the former operating theatre!

SCHAW HOUSE, BEARSDEN, GLASGOW

An outstanding property in the affluent Glasgow suburb of Bearsden, acquired by Premier Burrell as part of a portfolio of former nursing homes. The building, a James Thomson-designed 'mansion house', was presented to Glasgow Royal Infirmary on completion in 1895.

Replanned to provide 23 apartments and houses, the newly created homes generally take advantage of the magnificent views to the south. Most notable in the redesign is the centrally located top floor apartment incorporating a magnificent rooftop terrace.

E 52

Developer	The Burrell Company
Architect	MBLA
QS	Thomas & Adamson

Developer	The Burrell Company
Architect	Elder & Cannon Architects
QS	CRGP

Developer	Premier Burrell Ltd
Architect	Smith Scott Mullan Associates
QS	Pottie Wilson
Engineer	Will Rudd Davidson

Developer	Premier Burrell Ltd
Architect	Davis Duncan Architects
QS	Thomas & Adamson
Engineer	Woolgar Hunter

2006-

2006-

2006

2006-

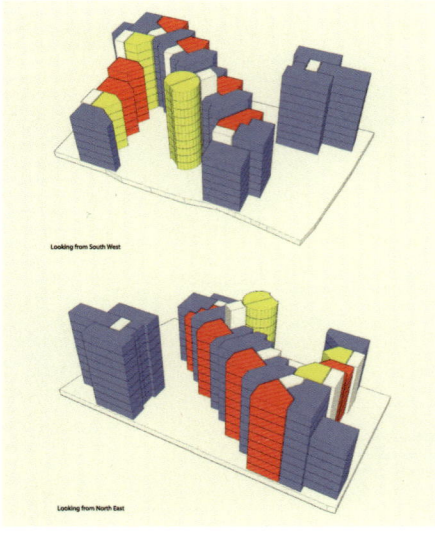

CHALMERS STREET, EDINBURGH

This unsuccessful proposal sought to build new housing on a car park site overlooking the Meadows, a central Edinburgh park. The intention was to match the new heights demonstrated in the neighbouring Royal Infirmary regeneration – Quartermile. The planning authority engaged fully with the proposals, seeking a street aligned four-storey tenement, preferably in sandstone.

FORMER HIGH SCHOOL, DALKEITH

In this joint effort with Wimpey, Buredi propose converting the two Listed former schools to apartments. The design, with Reiach and Hall Architects, acknowledges the rigour of the original layout of the school, and creates light and airy apartments.

TRON HOUSING, EDINBURGH

The final building in the Tron Regeneration provides affordable housing for Castle Rock Housing Association in a building that occupies the former site of the Nursery School. The commercial accommodation on the ground floor activates the street.

HIGH STREET, ABERDEEN

Working together with the University of Aberdeen this proposal brings some much needed buzz back into the heart of the Old Town, itself the centre of University life. Listed buildings fronting the High Street and overlooking King's College Chapel are retained and converted to a series of retail spaces whilst the derelict courtyard to the rear is opened up as a café / bar / restaurant with indoor and outdoor eating facilities.

E 53

E 54

Developer	The Burrell Company
Architect	Richard Murphy Architects

Developer	Buredi with Wimpey
Architect	Reiach & Hall Architects
QS	Faithful and Gould
Engineer	Harley Haddow

Developer	Castle Rock Housing Asssociation
Architect	Richard Murphy Architects
QS	Pottie Wilson
Engineer	Harley Haddow

Developer	The Burrell Company / University o f Aberdeen
Architect	David Murray Associates
QS	Murray Montgomery & Partners

2007-   2007-   2007-   2007-

PITSLIGO, EDINBURGH

This building in the Grange/Morningside area of Edinburgh is a former telephone exchange which has been redesigned by Broadway Malyan Architects, to form apartments and houses. The scheme also includes a small terrace of newbuild houses onto Clifton Drive. Large trees in mature grounds provide a magnificent setting for this reinvigorated residential block.

QUEEN'S HOTEL, GULLANE

This derelict Listed hotel on Gullane Main Street was under threat of demolition. Its proposed conversion to residential apartments is cross-funded by a new build terrace of houses tucked in to the rear. Although the proposals were challenged by a myriad of planning legislation the concensus is that it makes sense.

BROOMHILL HOUSE, KIRKINTILLOCH

One of a number of projects introduced to the group with the merging of Burrell and John Sheridan's Classical House. Broomhill is another conversion of a former hospital to apartments. This project will be carried out in association with Gladedale.

AULD WHARRIE, DUNBLANE

Conversion of an A Listed building to four houses. WIth architects Simpson & Brown, this project sees Burrell almost getting back to basics with this challenging conversion. The original design by George Walton includes some very fine interiors.

E 55

Developer	The Burrell Company	*Developer*	Premier Burrell Ltd	*Developer*	Classical Burrell	*Developer*	The Burrell Company
Architect	Broadway Malyan	*Architect*	Coast Architects	*Architect*	JM Architects	*Architect*	Simpson & Brown Architects
QS	SRC	*QS*	Cobb & Blyth	*QS*	CDP	*QS*	SRC
Engineer	PWP Consulting	*Engineer*	PWP Consulting	*Engineer*	CDP	*Engineer*	Wren & Bell

PUBLICATIONS AND EVENTS

PROSPECT ARTICLE
1987

Written by Forbes a year before he joined Burrell and carried in Prospect in 1987, this article created a heated response from Andy Doolan. The article illustrated the very healthy portfolio of Burrell projects.

Messrs Burrell and Doolan were still wrestling their way through a difficult split, with each of their new companies trying to outdo the other. Burrell had already started and this article caught the optimism of the time.

Andy Doolan's grand ventures in Glasgow following on from Ingram Square, were not progressing as he had hoped, with Cochrane Street being acquired by another developer.

BUSINESS SCOTLAND
1987

This early advert design promoted the Company's approach to urban regeneration. An approach that has now become commonplace – salvage, restore, revitalise, rather than clear away to start again. The Company 'mantra' of *Property Development by Design* seemed to be lost from later literature, although was clearly ever present in the body of work.

BURRELL CALENDAR
1990

Designed by Graphic Partners, this annual issue proved quite popular, and was immediately recognised on desks and in offices around the country. It was what Burrell referred to as 'an instant erection' – it arrived flat-packed, and sprang into form once removed from the envelope. The marbling and cracked finish demonstrates that this particular model was from the height of the Post-Modern period.

BURRELL BROCHURE
1995

Coming out of the recession in the 90s, it was important to promote. We felt we needed a Big Brochure. Graven Images worked with Burrell to create an unmissable production that probably didn't create any work for the company!

Shona Reid, then Head of the Scottish Arts Council, described it as extremely successful, only in that it was too big to go on a shelf or even in the bin so instead it lay on the floor, and had to be continually stepped over! It certainly got noticed.

The big idea had further problems. The cardboard box it was delivered in was far too big for most letter boxes.

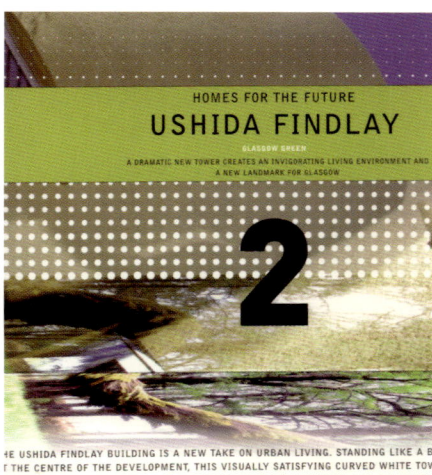

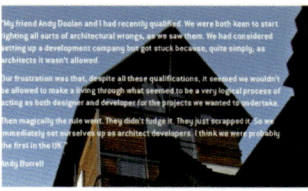

THE OTHER BURRELL COLLECTION
1996

One of Burrell's promotional ideas was to hold a small exhibition/reception to showcase the portfolio of past, current and future projects.

In essence a good idea, but as usual the amount of work required to create the exhibition panels was grossly underestimated. Held in the Mathew Gallery, it was a significant event, marking the achievement of moving on from the end of the recession. Perhaps due to the availability of free champagne, the reception was probably the most popular ever held in the Gallery, with queues forming along the street.

HOMES FOR THE FUTURE
SALES PARTICULARS
1999

The brief was to design a set of sales particulars that aspired to the same level of design as the buildings. Deyan Sudjic, Director of Glasgow 1999, was keen to hit new standards in all facets of design for the Expo. Tank were the chosen designers. The graphics arrived wrapped up in foil similar to a microwave oven meal!

SCOTTISH EXECUTIVE
'DESIGNING PLACES'
2001

The Glasgow Tower was a Burrell idea, then a competition with the GDA. As with so many other publications, Burrell's work or influence in Scotland is manifest. Burrell schemes have been used liberally in certain Planning Handbooks by authorities who often reject new Burrell proposals. It is, perhaps, understandable that people are willing to take plaudits after the hard work is done. However, the same individuals seem uneasy about initiating the process and sharing the vision and responsibility of change.

BURRELLOPOLIS EXHIBITION
25 YEARS OF THE BURRELL COMPANY
2007

The Lighthouse was chosen as the venue to celebrate Burrell's 25 years in architecture and property development. Designed with Graven Images, who carried out much of Burrell's early design work, the exhibition also celebrated the launch of this book.

INDEX

The Burrell Company
174 High Street
The Royal Mile
Edinburgh EH1 1QS
t +44 (0) 131 220 3040
f +44 (0) 131 220 2545

29 Park Circus
Glasgow G3 6AP
t +44 (0)141 332 6611
f +44 (0) 141 333 9966

e info@theburrellcompany.co.uk
w www.theburrellcompany.co.uk